$22.76

po 74601

1-10-01

The ebay Phenomenon

The ebay Phenomenon

BUSINESS SECRETS BEHIND THE WORLD'S HOTTEST INTERNET COMPANY

David Bunnell
CEO/EDITOR, UPSIDE MEDIA

With Richard A. Luecke

John Wiley & Sons, Inc.
New York • Chichester • Weinheim • Brisbane • Singapore • Toronto

Published by John Wiley & Sons, Inc.
Published simultaneously in Canada.

This publication is designed to provide accurate and authoritative information in regard to the subject matter covered. It is sold with the understanding that the publisher is not engaged in rendering legal, accounting, or other professional services. If legal advice or other expert assistance is required, the services of a competent professional person should be sought.

Library of Congress Cataloging-in-Publication Data:
Bunnell, David.
    The e-Bay phenomenon: business secrets behind the world's hottest Internet company / by David Bunnell with Richard A. Luecke.
        p.   cm.
    Includes bibliographical references and index.
    ISBN 0-471-38490-9 (cloth : alk. paper)
    1. Internet auctions.   I. Luecke, Richard A.   II. Title.
HF5478 B86 2000
381'.17'02854678—dc21   00-042271

Printed in the United States of America.

10 9 8 7 6 5 4 3 2 1

Contents

Preface

In January 2000, registered users of eBay, the world's most popular online auction site, received a communiqué from its CEO, Meg Whitman. "1999 was a historic year," she wrote, "filled with astonishing growth and rapid change." She went on to explain that the company had begun the year with a community of users roughly equal to the population of Portland, Oregon—about 2.2 million. By year-end, that number had grown to over 10 million, more than the population of Michigan. The site had generated more economic activity than any other Internet site.

Since it began operating in 1995, this company has produced revenues that most enterprises must labor decades to achieve, and has achieved a market value that exceeds those of Disney and dozens of other blue-chip companies. It has also produced that rarest of all e-business commodities: real profits.

eBay's remarkable growth has created a wide-ranging constituency of users, shareholders, business partners, and eBay watchers. Chances are that you belong to one of these groups. Or perhaps you are simply interested in the growing Internet economy and the phenomenal growth of one of its most visible pioneers. Whatever your interest, eBay's is a compelling and instructive business story. From small beginnings and modest goals, its business volume has exploded, and its name is becoming a household word. It has forged strategic relationships with America Online, Disney, and many lesser-known entities. And hardly a week goes by without its name appearing in a major business or general-interest publication.

The remarkable thing about this story is the extent to which the company and its people have managed these feats without a formal script. Because the person-to-person online auction market was virtually nonexistent in 1995, there was no blueprint to follow. Even now, each new day brings new opportunities and unforeseeable developments to which its management must respond—and quickly. The challenges are many and unique to the new medium of online person-to-person business: Hackers overload the company's servers, effectively blacking out the site; religious leaders scream bloody murder when someone decides to auction Nazi memorabilia; a rival begins "crawling" the company's site, capturing its data, and listing eBay auctions on its own site.

The list goes on and on.

With no road map to follow, eBay executives and employees have had to invent this business on the fly—in "Internet time." As a result, its evolution has been a consequence of strategic intention, reaction, and opportunistic response to unfolding events.

Other aspects of its development involve the adaptation of traditional business activities to the new world of e-commerce. These include brand development, customer acquisition and retention, outsourcing of key functions, and strategic alliances. Which is why the company is so fascinating.

The chapters that follow reveal eBay's origins, the community of users it has created, how its business model works, the competition it faces, and where it stands in the new online auction economy. You'll also learn about the people responsible for this phenomenon—both company employees and the world-spanning community of buyers and sellers who trade on the eBay site. Quite a few of the latter are small-business people who have used the site to make their enterprises larger, more interesting, and more profitable.

Several chapters end with very explicit lessons that business managers in the old economy and the new can contemplate and—hopefully—from which they can benefit.

Perhaps the greatest challenge I faced in developing this book was the fact that eBay's is an unfolding story. Every few days brought some significant announcement that forced me to go back and rewrite or add to chapters I thought were in the can: an acquisition, the introduction of an important new auction category, expansion into another national market, a hacker attack, the stock market tumble that took the company's share price down by roughly 44 percent in less than five weeks. Imagine painting a picture of a baseball game in progress and you'll appreciate what I had to contend with in writing these chapters.

The real mindblower came just a few weeks prior to the publisher's deadline for submitting the manuscript. That's when eBay and Yahoo! began a series of closed-door talks. These produced mountains of speculation. Would eBay sell out? Would the two e-giants enter into a strategic alliance? These questions remained unanswered even as I mailed off these chapters to the publisher, knowing full well that the printed book wouldn't hit the streets for another six months or so.

So, some of what you'll find here is bound to be superseded by events. But other things, such as the company's approach to managing hypergrowth and the lessons derived from eBay's relationship with its user community, will hopefully be of lasting value to readers.

Acknowledgments

Many individuals contributed their observations and insights to this book: consultants, e-commerce and securities analysts, eBay suppliers, fellow journalists, and eBay users. Many thanks are due to Geoffrey James and Mike Malone; John Perry Barlow of the Electronic Frontier Foundation; John Pecoraro and Prabakar Sundarrajan of Exodus Communications; Benchmark Capital's Bob Kagle; Michael May of Jupiter Communications; Forrester Research analyst Evie Black Dykema; David Morrison of Mercer Management Consulting; John Parkinson of Ernst & Young LLP; Julie Ward of Gomez.com; Dan Neary of AuctionWatch; Jamie Kiggen of Donaldson, Lufkin & Jenrette; and Tuck Rickards of Russell Reynolds Associates.

Special thanks are due to the many eBay users who, through e-mails and phone interviews, shared their experiences, their successes and their challenges as active eBaysians—in particular, Steve Barr of Barr's Fiddle Shop, Nigel Carroll of International Classic Cars, Larry (aka wishmaker), Kathleen (aka kleodnile), and Shirley Bryant (aka aaabooks).

Thanks also to my editor, Jeanne Glasser of John Wiley & Sons, who encouraged the development of this book, and to Richard Luecke of Salem, Massachusetts, who collaborated with me in the research and development of the manuscript.

The eBay Phenomenon

Frank Miller, a retired high school English teacher, had lots of stuff he no longer wanted, including various memorabilia he had collected over the years: books and old magazines; signatures of politicians, actors, and poets. He'd enjoyed having these things around his apartment. They were like old friends. But it was now time to part company and pass these old companions on to someone else. But how could he divest himself of these special things—and maybe pick up some extra money?

Frank didn't know a Word.doc from a dot-com, but a friend of his did and suggested auctioning off certain items on eBay. This friend, whose online user name was oscarwildcat, had just made his first purchase on the site and encouraged Frank to give it a try. "I've never sold anything on eBay," he told Frank, "but I'll auction your things if you'd like. It might be fun." Frank was game.

Getting the first item listed, a signed 1941 letter from

FDR's son James Roosevelt was anything but fun. Oscar hunted around for the right auction category to list it under. With thousands available on eBay, it wasn't obvious where this item should go. And it had to be in a category where potential buyers would find it. Eventually he settled on "Collectibles-Autographs-Political" as the right category and wrote up a description:

JAMES ROOSEVELT White House Letter

From the White House. James Roosevelt, FDR's son. Original signed letter on White House stationery. Dated 22 September 1941. To Mr. Sidney Katzman of Girard College, Philadelphia.

Good condition. Slight crease, and slight yellowed. Buyer to pay for 2-day UPS letter shipping.

He continued down eBay's online selling tool, clicking off his location, a minimum bid ($3), the length of the auction period (5 days), the forms of payment he'd accept (money order, cashier's check, or personal check), and other choices. "This is easy," he told himself.

Then he got to the picture. Everything he'd heard and read told him that bidders opened their wallets wider when they could see the goods. "Makes sense," he told himself as he scanned the Roosevelt letter into a JPEG file on his hard drive.

But now what? Somehow he had to upload this JPEG to a location on the Web, and then link it to the Roosevelt auction. Following eBay's seller instructions, he surfed over to www.pongo.com, a pay-for-space uploader. For 50 cents per file, Pongo would give him his own little spot in cyberspace—and the first three uploads were free! "I'm practically finished," he thought as the Pongo site flashed *Your upload is successful.*

One thing remained to be done: Link the uploaded JPEG to the listing and fire it off to eBay. Twenty minutes later, Oscar was still trying to make the link and was getting more and more frustrated. Fortunately, his wife, a person who believed in reading instructions *carefully,* was in the room. Within a moment she had resolved the problem and made the link. A few minutes later, the Roosevelt letter appeared on the eBay site, where millions of users in North America and around the world could see it and bid on Frank Miller's small artifact of American history. With the picture-linking problem resolved, Oscar was able to quickly list five more of Frank's items:

- A signed letter from then-Congresswoman Clare Booth Luce
- Autographed photos of Newt Gingrich and Dan Rostenkowski
- The Playbill from Neil Simon's *Jake's Women,* autographed by cast member Alan Alda
- The official press kit issued by Miramax films in connection with its release of *Shakespeare in Love,* complete with color slides and 8-by-10 glossies
- The game program from the 1926 football matchup between Stanford and the University of California

"Nothing to do now but wait for the bids to come in," Oscar told Frank over the phone the next morning.

■ EBAY AS A WAY OF LIFE

Frank and Oscarwildcat are just two of the millions of users scattered across the world who have made eBay a phenomenon in the expanding universe of e-commerce. For them, eBay auctions provide a convenient, efficient, and entertaining marketplace in which to sell and to shop. Though most users are casual participants who log on intermittently during the week to seek out bargains or find items for their personal collections, many have made eBay an important part of their lives and businesses.

Consider Shirley Bryant of Muskogee, Oklahoma. For years, Shirley operated a shop in Boulder, Colorado, featuring first-edition books. But even with a printed mail-order catalog she found that most of her customers lived within a two-hour drive of the shop. Beginning in the fall of 1997, Shirley began listing her more expensive books on eBay auctions. To her surprise and delight, items that would normally linger for months in her store sold quickly and at good prices. Better still, her local business took on global proportions. She was soon dealing with buyers from all over the United States, Japan, South Africa, Australia, and parts of Europe. "You get access to a customer base you'd never have through a catalog or store."

Thanks to eBay, Shirley has been able to relocate to her hometown of Muskogee, Oklahoma, where her operating expenses are one-third those in pricey Boulder. Today, eBay accounts for over half of her sales. "I just love eBay," says Shirley. "It has opened up a whole new sales avenue for me."

■ THE EBAY PHENOMENON

From its origin as a home business of founder Pierre Omidyar ("o-*mid*-ee-yar"), the company has become the world's leading auction market and one of a handful of major dotcom companies to actually turn a profit. Its growth has been nothing short of explosive since 1996, the year in which it reorganized as a corporation. And registered eBay user numbers have skyrocketed, growing to 10 million by the end of 1999. On an average day, 1.8 million unique visitors enter the site. Every second, five items are listed for sale on eBay—that translates to $113 of gross merchandise sales *every second*.

At any given time, Web surfers can find over 4 million

items in over 2,000 different product categories on eBay. In calendar year 1999, 129.6 million items were listed, and at $2.8 billion in 1999 (Figure 1.1), gross merchandise sales topped those of any other Internet site, making it the world's largest market for person-to-person online trading. Jupiter Communications estimates that eBay controls 94 percent of the *existing* person-to-person online auction market, a market that is anticipated to grow substantially in the years ahead.

According to a 1999 report issued by Forrester Research, spending on person-to-person auction sites like eBay is predicted to grow to $6.4 billion by 2004. Some portion of that growth will likely come from traditional person-to-person trading forums—classified ads, collectibles shows, and auction houses—which are estimated to exceed $100 billion in the United States alone. Many items traditionally listed in classified ads or sold at flea markets, estate sales, and tradi-

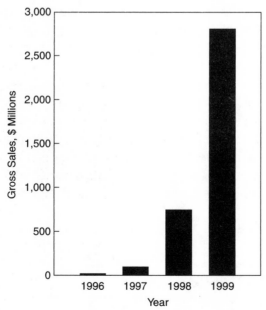

Figure 1.1 Gross merchandise sales on the eBay site, 1996–1999.

tional live auctions are already finding buyers online. The reason, as Shirley Bryant and thousands of others have discovered, is that online auctions enormously expand the geographic reach of sellers. And with more buyers available, sellers have a higher probability of obtaining higher prices.

Shoppers, too, like online auctions. Have you ever tried to track down Volume 3 of a multivolume chronicle of World War II? Finding it can mean endless hours of schlepping around to flea markets, used bookstores, and garage sales. Go online and the odds of success turn in your favor. In just a few seconds, an auction site search engine can sort through thousands of books and take you to *exactly* what you want. If Volume 3 is there, you'll know it in an instant. You may find that 10 sellers are offering Volume 3, some in better condition than others. Put in a bid, and you may get the one you want.

eBay isn't simply the biggest of the online sites, it's also one of the most appealing to consumers and corporate partners. In company with Yahoo! and Microsoft Network, it received a Media Matrix/Industry Standard award as a "best all-around" Web site. It ranked fifth among the most popular of *all* Internet sites in terms of the number of unique visitors who clicked on it during 1999, and first in terms of "most engaging." Even more impressive, eBay visitors spent an average of 105 minutes per month at the site, nearly 20 percent more than the second-place finisher (FreeRide.com).[1] And in the quarterly rating published by Gomez.com, it consistently captures the highest overall score, and is rated number one from the perspective of all key user groups: bargain hunters, hobbyists and collectors, and sellers.

■ EBAY AND THE NEW WORLD OF E-COMMERCE

eBay is just one of many important players in an expanding e-commerce industry. Estimates of the size of that industry in the United States alone, its rate of growth, and the number of Internet users are widely scattered—primarily because of how *user* is defined. Researchers like International Data Corporation (IDC), CyberDialogue, Forrester Research, CommerceNet, and Jupiter Communications all have their own estimates and growth forecasts. There is no way of proving who's on target, and being on the money probably isn't even important, since everyone agrees on two things: E-commerce is big, and it is getting bigger very fast.

Consider the number of people who surf the Internet. If you simply took an average of the number of U.S. Internet users estimated by the research firms just mentioned, you'd have 83.5 million users in 1999, with an average forecast of 143 million by 2003—more than half of the adult U.S. population. Research indicates that 40 percent of those users are college graduates with substantial household incomes. Web use outside the United States is less intense, but it's picking up momentum, and IDC estimates that the number of Web users will grow to approximately 500 million worldwide by year-end 2003.

If the number of Internet-connected people is growing, the magnitude of business conducted by the average user should grow even faster. There is simply more to be purchased over the Net every year, both by consumers and businesses. A few years ago, e-tailer sites were few, and people who would routinely give a credit-card number over the phone to a catalog sales rep were terrified about using plastic to buy a flannel shirt over the Net from squeaky-clean L.L. Bean. Today, Internet surfers have lost that fear, and they can now buy everything from airline tickets to prescription drugs to groceries to automobiles online. And they're doing it in greater and greater numbers. From less than $8 billion in 1998, Forrester Research predicts that online retail sales will reach $108 billion by 2003—that's about 6 percent of all forecasted U.S. retail sales.

Retail sales on the Net get most of the headlines, but the business-to-business (B2B) segment of e-commerce,

---

THE BIGGEST DAY

The biggest single day of online consumer business as of this writing occurred on December 14, 1999, when, according to BizRate.com, consumers placed 2.5 million online merchandise orders worth more than $240 million.

---

estimated at $114 billion in 1999 by Goldman Sachs, has far outpaced consumer transactions. B2B is forecasted to dominate online sales in the years ahead, representing 70 to 75 percent of all online transactions. The effects of this form of commerce should be good for the economy as a whole. According to the Federal Reserve Bank of New York, the shift from traditional to online B2B commerce will lead to lower prices, greater productivity, and reduced labor costs.

All told, B2B, business-to-consumer (B2C), and person-to-person (P2P) e-commerce may approach $400 billion in 2003. Again, there are wide projection variations, if only because a universally accepted definition of *e-commerce* is hard to come by.[2]

➤ The Explosive Online Auction Economy

eBay participates in the *demand-based* or *dynamic pricing* segment of online commerce. There, transaction prices are determined entirely by buyers. This is fundamentally different from what most of us are accustomed to. Usually, vendors make the pricing decisions, and we either accept their prices or look elsewhere for a better deal. In demand-based pricing, buyers make these critical decisions.

The auction is the most familiar form of demand-based pricing. Auction forums have been around since ancient times, and everything from foodstuffs, minerals, timber, animals, securities, and human beings have been bought and sold through them.

Bringing the auction online was an important innovation, and is one of the greatest uses of Internet technology. The Internet has facilitated a variety of commercial activities. Many are lifted directly from offline models and provide no greater value or convenience for customers. Ordering a pair of gloves from an e-tail site is a prime example. From the customer's perspective, this is neither cheaper nor more convenient than buying the same gloves from the retailer's catalog using an 800 number. Online auctions, in contrast, have created something very new. Michael May, auction analyst for Jupiter Communications, views them as an ideal use of the Internet as a medium. "Of all the things you can do with the Internet," he noted in our interview, "this is one of the great ones. The resources necessary to launch and maintain this type of business, and the risks associated with it, are tiny compared with other online retail operations. And the cost of goods sold is simply the cost of transferring information electronically."

Many see the origins of online auction business in Priceline.com, which went on the Internet in 1995. Priceline created a *reverse* auction, a system through which buyers specify the amount they are willing to pay for a generic product or service—for example, an airline ticket between Chicago and Los Angeles, or a hotel room in New York City. If one of Priceline's sellers is willing to let its product or service go at that price, a transaction takes place. Both parties benefit from this type of transaction. The buyer gets a low price, and the seller unloads something that might otherwise expire as worthless. Because, according to Priceline, airlines fly with over 500,000 seats empty every day, and thousands of hotel rooms are vacant every night, any sale that covers the cost of the airline's snack food or the hotel's cost of cleaning a room contributes to profits and overhead, and is worth taking.

Since its introduction, Priceline has extended its offerings to other categories: home mortgages, cars, and even groceries (through WebHouse). By early 2000 it aimed to follow with other "perishables" such as rental cars and cruise ship vacations.

Priceline provides a venue for demand-based pricing, but it is not an auction in which many buyers can bid against each other. That changed in 1995, when eBay (then AuctionWeb) went online. Other sites soon followed.

➤ Different Types of Online Auctions

Banking on the enormous number of Internet users who pass through their sites, Yahoo! and Amazon both entered the fray with auction formats strikingly similar to eBay's (more on these in Chapter 8). Others were less ambitious and were category specific: Guitarauction.com, BabyBid .com (no, you cannot buy a child here, but you can bid for baby and children's items), AntiquePhotos.com, and dozens more. Many readers are probably familiar with these P2P sites, and may even have bought or sold things through them. Less visible is the much larger B2B side of the online auction world—which, according to Forrester Research, may grow to $52.6 billion in transactions by 2002. B2B auctions are now available for a wide variety of industries and goods. Many are highly specialized. AssetLine accepts online bids for construction, manufacturing, and transportation equipment. bLiquid.com features online auctions for industrial equipment and supplies. TexEx.com provides a site where textile companies can buy or sell raw materials peculiar to their industry. The exchange site announced in February 2000 by General Motors, Ford, and DaimlerChrysler is anticipated to handle auto component and materials transactions totaling $500 billion per year.

The attraction of online B2B sites to industrial companies is powerful, and they are making our economy more efficient. Consider the personal computer industry. Most PCs and peripherals are now configured from standardized components. On any given day, hundreds of electronics companies are overstocked on certain of these components, while hundreds of others are short of the same items. Online auction sites that bring these industry participants together efficiently and in real time provide a cost-saving solution. Selling companies are able to unload unneeded inventory, while others can quickly locate the components they need—often at bargain prices. Both parties reduce their costs, and the savings are eventually divided between shareholders and end-use consumers.

FastParts.com is a good example of a B2B auction site in action. Founded in 1991 to bring buyers and sellers of semiconductors and other electronic parts together, the company took its trading floor online in 1996. It describes itself as a spot market where original equipment manufacturers, contract manufacturers, distributors, and part makers buy and sell electronic parts at market-driven prices. Trading is conducted anonymously between prequalified site members. Some trades are accomplished through auction, and others through a trading exchange patterned after the NASDAQ model used in the securities industry. In both instances, prices are driven by supply and demand, with FastParts compensating itself with a small percentage of each transaction.

Components and raw materials are not the only items found on these B2B auctions. A new site, Bid4geek.com, deals exclusively in human commerce. No, this is not a modern-day slave auction, but a place where human resource managers can check out and acquire technical personnel. "Welcome to a new way of finding and securing the best high-tech talent on the Internet," it proclaims. "This site was created with the geek in mind, which means you'll have access to the best IT [information technology] talent around."

Together, P2P, B2C, and B2B auctions and demand-based exchanges are taking a larger and larger chunk of total e-commerce. One industry watcher, Keenan Vision, estimates that the various types of demand-based-pricing transactions will represent roughly one-third of all online transactions by 2002.

➤ Big Economic Benefits

The growth of market-pricing transactions is bound to make our economy more efficient, and nowhere more so than in the realm of person-to-person and small dealer-to-person exchanges of goods, which are chronically inefficient. In strictly economic terms, markets are *efficient* when the following conditions are met:

- The features of goods are fairly standard.
- Buyers and sellers are many.
- Information about the goods being offered is widely shared.
- Asking and bidding prices are not far apart.

Modern financial markets provide our best examples of market efficiency. In a transaction involving 100 shares of IBM common stock, for example, the features of those shares are identical. On any given day, thousands of individuals and institutions are buying and selling. All buyers and sellers have access to the same information about IBM's current business situation. So, as the many buyers and sellers of IBM common stock congregate around the company's trading post on the floor of the New York Stock Exchange, competition and shared information has the effect of bringing the prices asked and offered very close together—say, $121 to sell and $120¼ to buy. Generally, buyers and sellers meet near the middle. Everything happens quickly, efficiently, and with relatively little "friction," or trading costs.

The current retail market for automobiles is less perfect, but still qualifies as an efficient marketplace. The features of the various models are generally standard, and pricing can be readily adjusted to recognize unique features, such as sun roofs, high and low engine mileage, standard versus automatic transmissions, and so forth. Auto sellers and buyers are both numerous, eliminating the ability of any individual participant to exercise monopolistic pricing power. Finally, information about new and used automobiles is abundant and widely available. Thanks to the Internet and print publications like *Consumer Reports,* anyone hunting for the best buy on a particular new car model can easily determine the dealer's invoice cost, the dealer cost of different options, and the offering prices of dozen of competing sellers. Equally useful information is available on used cars.

The upshot of the market characteristics just described is that you're not likely to be screwed when you go out to buy a car—there are simply too many sellers and too much easily obtained information. If you are taken to the cleaners, you have no one to blame but yourself. On the flip side, the opportunity to screw the auto dealer is equally limited, since there are plenty of other potential buyers out there, and sellers have lots of information. This is market efficiency. Market efficiency has the beneficial effect of bringing selling and bidding prices closer together, and closer to *true* values.

Traditional person-to-person markets, in contrast, are highly inefficient. They are geographically fragmented, making it difficult for buyers and sellers to meet and do business. Transaction costs are high. Pricing benchmarks are difficult or impossible to find. If, for example, you are looking for a selection of Big Bopper albums, your only chance of hitting pay dirt is to comb through used record stores in a wide geographic area—a time-consuming process. The probability of finding the specific recordings you want through flea markets or classified ads is even more remote. And if you somehow luck out and find someone selling a Big Bopper album, you will have no reference point for pricing. The seller will be equally challenged; finding and connecting with you will be difficult and expensive, especially if he or she has to resort to classified ads.

The beauty of eBay's vision is that it has eliminated many of the inefficiencies of traditional person-to-person commerce. It provides a place where buyers and sellers can conveniently meet, exchange information about goods and prices, and transact sales at minimum costs. And it has made collecting and bargain hunting fun.

One organization that has benefited from this more efficient market is the State of Oregon Property Distribution Center.[3] By Oregon statute, recovered property and goods confiscated from drug dealers and other ne'er-do-wells belong to the state. Consequently, Oregon owns at any given time an assortment of odd merchandise that it must get rid of: shampoo, electric drills, computers, mountain bikes, gold rings and chains (street gang favorites), atmospheric monitors, porcelain dolls, umbrellas (listed as "Oregon winter survival gear"), snowboards, comic book collections, live cattle, and, on one occasion, a white leather halter top and vest. The agency's description of this last set of items is enough to make some healthy males faint:

> The items included in this sale are offered by a local police agency having been obtained as a result of civil forfeiture and/or other criminal activity.
>
> This lot contains a couple of real flashy leather garments!
> 1–White Leather Halter Top, Extra Small, Wilson's Leather, NEW!
> 1–Genuine Leather Vest by H.L. Spencer Limited, Natural/Tobacco in Color, NEW!

In the past, this state agency unloaded its goods through the usual channels: sealed bids, fixed price sales, general store sales, and public auctions. But when you think about it, how much would a proper Oregonian pay for a slutty leather halter top? Surely it would fetch twice as much in New Jersey. So the agency set itself up on eBay under the user name oregontrail 2000, an auction site described by one eBayer as "better than Wal-Mart." It now has a much larger pool of potential buyers and is pulling down much better prices for its property.

➤ A Slice of the Big Pie

The slice of the online auction market occupied by eBay had lots of growth potential ahead as this book went to press, but most analysts at the time were already describing its limits. Forrester's Evie Black Dykema predicted that consumer-oriented demand-driving pricing models would capture only a small percentage of total Web sales by 2004. "Bargain hunting is a hobby, not a way of life," she wrote. "By 2003, only 22 percent of all online shoppers will religiously take the time to shop around. . . . And they will only do it for big-ticket, researched purchases like stereos and home theater systems—not cheap, easy-to-find products like corn-flakes."[4]

But even a small percentage of a huge number translates into major business potential, and eBay is well situated to

---

FRANK AND OSCAR REVISITED

The morning after Oscar listed Frank Miller's six auction items, he surfed to his eBay page to check the number of incoming bids. Nothing! This was disappointing, but he had heard that the real action happens only when auctions are in their final days or hours.

By the next afternoon, things were looking better—a number of bids had floated in, though not more than a few dollars each. As the days passed and the auctions entered their final hours, the bids came in faster and rose as buyers

(Continues)

(*Continued*)

competed with each other. When it was all over, the Roosevelt letter drew a disappointing final bid—only about $15—but the buyer was happy as a clam. "My father loves history and politics," she wrote. "He'll love this." Other items did much better than expected. The *Shakespeare in Love* press kit attracted a $35 winning bid, and the UC–Stanford 1926 football program garnered $152.

After he deducted his eBay fees and image-hosting charges, Oscar was able to send Frank a $247 check for things that had been sitting around Frank's apartment gathering dust.

grab the lion's share of it. And though bargain hunting may be a hobby, it has created a vast community of eBay users. How the company latched onto that market and how it developed as a business entity is the subject of the next chapter.

Chapter

Pierre Omidyar Starts a Company

■ THE LITTLE COMPANY THAT CAME OUT OF NOWHERE
■ TWO KEY DECISIONS SPELLED SUCCESS ■ THE REWARDS
OF ENTREPRENEURSHIP ■ "WE ARE A COMMUNITY"

The business world took a major change in direction when the computer came along—and thank God! If it hadn't, people like me—and maybe like you—would be toiling away at *regular* jobs—selling detergents, writing ad copy for a new brand of breath deodorant, or shuffling paper somewhere in the bowels of an old-line manufacturing company.

Mercifully, the computer revolution has saved many of us from all that. The biggest beneficiaries, of course, have been the techies who now have opportunities aplenty to earn big money and get some respect. Today, the individuals whom everyone in high school and college regarded as geeks, nerds, and propeller-heads are making big bucks as software developers, systems analysts, chip designers, Webmeisters, and even entrepreneurial superheroes. It's about time they had an opportunity to shine.

The computer revolution also ushered in totally new types of businesses based on the Internet. Here, one-time

GEEKS' NIGHT OUT

As a sign of their growing self-awareness and importance to American commerce, technogeeks in the Boston area annually celebrate their culture with Geek Pride Day and a festival at a swank Hub location. Here's how they described the April 2000 festivities on www.geekpride.org:

> An unabashed celebration of geekdom, vers. 1.0 of The Geek Pride Festival celebrates the victory of the geek: derided in high schools across America, now heralded as the engines of the new economy. Go figure? Go geek!

> The Festival is free. No charges for tickets, to hear a speaker, to hang with some friends. We are charging to use the bathrooms. They'll be $100 per use, with a 2-minute limit. We take Mastercard, Visa or fully vested stock options in pre-IPO companies with significant venture backing. . . . It would be kinda cool if geeks from all over this little old world of ours could take a couple days off to celebrate. What the hell!

One festival organizer summed up the new stature of geekdom this way in a radio interview: "Geeks are now running the world."

propeller-heads are prominent among the crown princelings. While the fortunes of hardware and software companies rise and fall on their ability to design, manufacture, and sell the most technically advanced products—real stuff—the success of the new dot-com companies depends on the appeal of their business designs and on their ability to execute those designs extremely well. Software and systems—geek specialties—are key parts of the execution equation. For example, Hewlett-Packard prospers to the extent that it can profitably crank out stuff with customer-pleasing features and improved performance at acceptable prices. The same goes for General Electric, Motorola, Intel, Citibank, and other giants of what everyone has already dubbed the *old economy*. Amazon.com, in contrast, has made its way in the world through the ability of its business design to add value to the product selection process, make ordering simple, and fill orders efficiently.

Like Dell, Gateway, and other companies that rely heavily on an Internet link to customers, Amazon's business design has two essential parts. The first is a self-service customer interface—its Web site—where buyers of books and other items can find, see, read about, and specify what they want. Consider the company's main product area—books. The customer interface for books is convenient, easy to use, and makes it possible to locate and purchase books in a lot less time than it takes to do so through a traditional retail bookstore—which might not even stock the desired publications. And the site is open 24 hours per day, every day. Amazon also provides value-adding features that brick-and-mortar competitors do not: book reviews, feedback from customers who have already read the books, and a short list (with links) of related books that customers might want to consider.

The customer interface is the easy part of Amazon's business design. Fulfillment—getting the right items to customers quickly and efficiently—is the most critical issue faced by Amazon and many other dot-com companies. Hidden behind the convenient interface we all see when we click onto Amazon.com is a complex supply network of publishers, book dealers, warehouses, and shippers. Building an efficient and effective network and orchestrating it to perform to its highest potential is the greatest challenge faced by that company's management. The cool Web site will not retain a customer if the fulfillment part of the business sends the wrong title, ships to the wrong address, or gets it there too late for Christmas.

After all, Barnesandnoble.com is just a click away. And brick-and-mortar stores are all over the map.

If the Internet has introduced a revolution in the pace and the manner in which we do business, the leaders of that revolution are people who introduce new business designs and make them work. Many are techies. And the most successful of these have good heads for business, or work closely with people who do. This combination of a powerful business design tailored to the Internet economy, a philosophy of openness and community, and business savvy came together in the company the world now knows as eBay.

■ THE LITTLE COMPANY THAT CAME OUT OF NOWHERE

Pierre Omidyar was born in Paris in 1968, and moved with his parents to Washington, D.C., while still a young boy. By the time he reached high school, the Apple II—the first practical personal computer—was being snapped up by technologists and hobbyists, and the IBM PC was just coming onto the market.

Like lots of kids, Omidyar developed a passion for computer programming and applied that passion to a most mundane task—computerizing the card catalog of his school library. He was paid $6 an hour for that little job, which must be less than what his current net worth earns in the blink of an eye. He pursued his interest at Tufts University, just outside Boston, where he earned an undergraduate degree in computer science, then joined Claris, a software subsidiary of Apple Computer, where he developed the popular MacDraw application.

E-commerce was a new idea back in 1991 when Omidyar cofounded Ink Development Corporation (later renamed eShop), one of the pioneers of online retailing. When Ink was bought out by Microsoft, he went on to work for General Magic, a mobile communication platform company, and was working there when the idea of online auctions cropped up.

Business in the Valley was at an important turning point back then. Pundits, analysts, and venture capitalists were turning their attention away from electronics manufacturers like Hewlett-Packard, the company that put the Valley on the map, and getting excited about the new companies on the block, the Internet-based start-ups.

Those newcomers stood on the shoulders of earlier hardware and software developers. Previous generations of Valley companies had developed and produced chips, central processing units (CPUs), printers, scanners, and servers—the "boxes" that powered the Computer Age. In contrast, the newcomers didn't make anything. Instead, they brought those inventions to the Web and married them to business models that promised to change the way people did business. The term *business model* gained the same currency with investors and analysts that technical breakthroughs in chip design had enjoyed in previous years.

A confluence of big money and big ideas for electronic commerce ignited a new generation of growth in Silicon Valley. Between 1986 and 1996, the pool of available venture capital roughly doubled. And the Internet seemed to offer even greater potential for changing peoples' lives and business behaviors than had the telephone, television, and other major technical advances.

Netscape Communications may have set the tone for "Silicon Valley II." Netscape was the ideal of the new entrepreneurs and the venture capitalists who supported them. Within 24 hours of its going public in August 1994, Netscape's share price doubled. And it kept on going, making multimillionaires of its founders, the venture capitalists, and scores of the young and inexperienced employees whom the gods of good fortune had placed on the payroll at the time. Jim Collins, who authored the best-selling business book (with Jerry Porras) *Built to Last* (Harper-

Collins, 1994), describes this new period in Silicon Valley history as the era of "Built to Flip." In this era, winning entrepreneurs were guided by a very different script than the one followed by Bill Hewlett and David Packard, William Boeing, Paul Galvin (Motorola), Sam Walton, Gordon Moore (Intel), and other company founders whom he'd researched. The new script was "Develop a good idea, raise venture capital, grow rapidly, and then go public or sell out—but above all, do it fast."[1]

This was the environment in which Pierre Omidyar had come of age, and on which he has now left his mark. But his company and its service—unlike many others—appealed equally to venture capitalists and real customers.

Silicon Valley lore maintains that Omidyar was inspired to start an online auction mechanism by his wife's (then girlfriend's) hobby of collecting Pez dispensers. The truth is that he had been thinking about such a venture before he was even aware of her Pez mania.

> I had been thinking about how to create an efficient marketplace—a level playing field, where everyone had access to the same information and could compete on the same terms as anyone else. Not just a site where big corporations sold stuff to consumers and bombarded them with ads, but rather one where people "traded" with each other. . . . I thought, if you could bring enough people together and let them pay whatever they thought something was worth . . . real values could be realized and it could ultimately be a fairer system—a win-win for buyers and sellers.[2]

That initial interest led to the creation of AuctionWeb, a home-based business with very limited expectations run by Omidyar and his partner, Jeff Skoll. Both thought it wise to keep their day jobs.

Unlike Omidyar, whose background was in computer science, Skoll was a Stanford MBA with substantial hands-on business experience, including work with Knight-Ridder's online information venture. Together, they made a perfect set of cyberentrepreneurs. Omidyar created a concept for serving people on the Internet, and Skoll had the know-how to turn that concept into a business—for structuring fees and systems and developing a market. In many respects, Skoll turned a project into a machine for making money.

➤ Small Beginnings

The new company was formed as a sole proprietorship in September 1995 and operated from Omidyar's small apartment, using a Web site provided by his Internet service provider (ISP). A filing cabinet, an old school desk, and a laptop computer were the tools of its makeshift trade. In order to develop a critical mass of transactions, users were charged no fees whatsoever, but within six months, the two entrepreneurs began charging token fees (25 cents per listing) with no larger goal than to cover their rising Internet service costs. Before long, however, traffic on this site was so intense that the ISP told Omidyar to take a hike. He had to buy his own server and install it in his apartment.

"People seemed happy to pay for the service," Omidyar reported later, "except I was so busy keeping the site going, I couldn't even get to the mail and open the checks that were piling up. That's when I realized my little hobby-experiment had taken on a life of its own."[3]

Omidyar and Skoll had, in fact, merely scratched the surface of a huge market—one that in the United States alone approached $100 billion in annual goods transactions through flea markets, public auctions, garage sales, and classified ads.[4] And beneath that mountain of sales was an even larger cache of potential value locked up and forgotten in attics and basements around the globe. The communicating power of the Internet made it possible for the first time to efficiently tap that huge market.

Mike S. Malone, now editor of *Forbes ASAP,* was a consultant to small start-ups in the San Francisco Bay area when Omidyar and Skoll were in the early stages of developing their business model. "They were young kids and they really weren't that different than other start-up teams I'd dealt with," he recalled in a March 2000 interview. "They had the same infinite enthusiasm and the belief that they would make it big that I'd seen in other start-ups. They were smart—but so was everybody out there. They were really hard workers—especially Jeff—but everyone was working his ass off. They, like lots of people, understood that the Internet would be huge."

The company incorporated in May 1996, but until July 1996 had no employees other than its founders, who paid themselves annual salaries of $25,000. Even so, business had grown to the point where Omidyar had to move the operation from his apartment to a one-room office in Sunnyvale and hire a part-time employee to handle the checks and billings. Employee number one was Chris Agarpao, whom Omidyar had met at a wedding, and who soon thereafter was interviewed at a picnic table on the grounds of Omidyar's apartment complex.

The odds against the success of this new venture would have seemed substantial back in 1995 and 1996. The market for the sale of goods over the Internet, particularly through person-to-person trading, was new, and did not enjoy widespread acceptance. Buying something of substantial value, often sight unseen, from a total stranger hundreds or thousands of miles away did not fall into the category of natural acts. Further, the growth of Internet use would have to continue if the auction market hoped to gain real size. And there was no assurance that it would. Public enthusiasm for Web surfing might stall out. Even if public acceptance was high, the network infrastructure needed to accommodate rapidly growing usage might not be forthcoming. More than a few pundits predicted that the network would collapse under the weight of growing consumer and business use. Higher levels of Internet usage might require new standard and protocols and broadband delivery. Insufficient infrastructure and high demand might slow the Internet and turn off users. Those were the logical macroconcerns. At the company level, you had to wonder what would happen if the company's servers crashed or if lots of auction participants started complaining of being ripped off.

There were also questions about the popularity of the items offered in eBay auctions. Future revenues depended on continuing demand for the types of goods listed by users of the service. For example, during April through June 1998, over 30,000 auctions were simultaneously listed in the "Beanie Babies" category. Trading in this one category, in fact, accounted for about 6 percent of eBay's revenues during that year. As most everyone knows, Beanie Babies are a deliberately manufactured collectible—and only Beanie Baby devotees can explain why they have any monetary value. Like Pet Rocks and Cabbage Patch Kids, the appeal of these items could quickly evaporate, reducing eBay's revenue.

Then, of course, there was the risk that America Online (AOL), Amazon, Yahoo!, or any of the full-grown gorillas of the Internet would see the same opportunity and wrestle it away from Omidyar and Skoll. No major barriers stood between those companies and market entry. If Omidyar and Skoll could do it on a shoestring, so could others. And many eventually did.

➤ **Enter the Venture Capitalists**

By the spring of 1997, the auction site was growing at a rapid clip and already had a handful of employees, mostly software and systems engineers, who busied themselves with back-office duties and customer service. Omidyar and Skoll recognized that additional capital and management expertise would be needed if they hoped to realize the full potential of their new enterprise. So one day Omidyar made a phone call to Bruce Dunlevie, a Silicon

Valley venture capitalist (VC) and partner in the then-new firm of Benchmark Capital. Benchmark's strategy was to be the first venture investor in technology companies that aimed to create new markets in a few broad areas: application services, consumer devices, data services, networking equipment, semiconductors, software, and the various segments of e-commerce.

Dunlevie and Omidyar had become acquainted several years earlier, when the latter was employed by eShop. Dunlevie was invited to come over and check out the new auction operation. When he did, he took along one of his partners, Bob Kagle, the Benchmark specialist in consumer-oriented e-commerce.

Like his other four partners, Kagle was young, tall, male, and energetic. With an average age of 36 and average height of 6-foot-3, Benchmark could have fielded a respectable basketball team. Kagle, a native of Flint, Michigan, with a Stanford MBA and experience with Boston Consulting Group, was immediately impressed by Omidyar's unassuming, even-keeled manner. "He had a high listen-to-talk ratio," he recalled, "and was keen on what was best for the company, even if it meant bringing in someone else to run it."[5]

During their first meeting, the VCs saw the Auction-Web site and were given a demo by Omidyar. "It wasn't the most elegant design," Kagle recalled in our interview. "It was basically black and white with Courier type on the listings."

Though the site was underwhelming, Dunlevie and Kagle were impressed by its results. Thousands of listed items were selling every day. The checks were coming in, and receipts exceeded expenses—a major miracle in the new world of e-commerce. A few weeks later, Dunlevie and Kagle checked again. To their delight, the number of listings and transactions had increased, and even more checks were coming in.

Kagle spent more time with Omidyar and Skoll, and observed how the metrics of the site improved from week to week with little or no intervention or effort. Some 50,000 items were then listed on the site on a daily basis, and monthly receipts were almost $200,000. The site had all the appearances of a money-making machine. Kagle wondered what would happen if someone actually made an effort to push things along.

Bob Kagle recalls what hooked him. It wasn't simply the profit potential; the site was lots of fun. "I got onto the site to explore one of my own passions, which is collecting antique fishing decoys. That's part of my Michigan heritage." Searching the site, he quickly found a good selection. "There were ten to fifteen of them [including] one from a famous carver in my hometown." Kagle made an offer on that item, but lost to a higher bidder. "But that experience helped me understand why eBay was such a powerful idea. It's fun!"

Person-to-person online trading was something new to Kagle, but he sensed something really big. "If you could enable a marketplace of person-to-person trading on a global basis, and make it effective and efficient, that was a big idea," he recounted. "What wasn't clear to me was how this early marketplace of collectors would translate into a practical business. How, for example, would people deal with things like automobiles, refrigerators, and furniture—items with substantial shipping requirements?" Nor was the extent to which online auctions could disintermediate traditional channels for noncollector person-to-person exchange—classified ads, garage sales, and regular auctions—apparent.

Only two months after first meeting with Omidyar and Skoll, Benchmark decided to provide early-stage financing to the tune of $5 million ($3 million initially). In return, Benchmark obtained stock and warrants representing 22 percent of the company. As we'll see later, Kagle was more fortunate in this transaction than in his failed bid to buy his fish decoy. He never got the decoy for his collection, but the decision to invest in eBay would make a multimillionaire of him and of each of his partners.

➤ Gearing Up

Omidyar's company continued to attract buyers and sellers almost exclusively through word of mouth. In September 1997, however, it began to court potential customers through banner ads on selected sites and ad placements in targeted publications. That same month it formally adopted the name *eBay* and launched a redesigned user interface and a new, scalable back-end transaction-processing architecture. By year-end it had expanded its total headcount to 41 and could boast 850,000 registered users and annual revenues of $340 million.

Ironically, the company never touched its venture capital as it continued to grow. Positive cash flow allowed it to self-finance its early-stage growth. Which begs the question: What did Omidyar and Skoll get for 22 percent of their company (an interest worth $2.5 billion at one point in the wake of the company's initial public offering [IPO])?

Omidyar and Skoll hadn't been looking solely for cash; they wanted help with building the business and recruiting talent capable of managing what they hoped would be a period of skyrocketing growth. Collaboration between entrepreneurs and venture capitalists had, in fact, been the catalytic agent that produced many of the most spectacular IPO outcomes of the past. "What is clear from our investigations," wrote Jeffry Timmons and William Bygrave in one of the few thorough studies of the venture capital industry, "is that the successful development of a business can be critically affected by the relationship between the venture capitalist and the management team. . . . When they are in synch, the results are often stunning."[6]

In many of the classic cases of great start-ups that go on to become great companies—Federal Express, Apple, Oracle, and others—venture capitalists brought more than money to the table. They introduced entrepreneurs to their networks of potential chief executive officers, marketing gurus, key suppliers, consultants, and bankers—which is what Benchmark aimed to do. Working with

Kagle, now a board member, and other Benchmark partners, the company began beating the bushes for top talent, both for the eBay corner office and for its key positions and board of directors.

➤ Finding the Right CEO

Generally, company founders retain the role of CEO and use it to guide the development of their companies, often for many years. Some have been remarkably successful in this role: Bill Gates, Scott McNealy of Sun Microsystems, Amazon's Jeff Bezos, and Michael Dell being prime examples.[7] These individuals developed executive skills as their companies grew. Each successfully made the transition from technical expert to capable manager and leader of a hugely expanding enterprise.

Not every start-up founder is capable of making that transition, but the idea of bringing in an outsider to run the business—their baby—is anathema to many entrepreneurs. Pierre Omidyar was not one of these. Those who know him describe him as mature, unassuming, and even-keeled, a man who wanted to do what was best for the company, even if it meant turning operational control over to someone else. Per Bob Kagle, "he was balanced in his view of what his own role had been and would be going forward." And he was keen on getting the very best people around him—people who could help the company realize its full potential. "It's rare to find someone that enlightened," says Kagle, who has worked with dozens of start-ups.

The CEO search eventually identified many talented and experienced executives, and half a dozen were contacted and interviewed. But, in the end, the choice came down to Meg Whitman.

➤ The Reluctant Recruit

Margaret C. (Meg) Whitman was 40 years old when she was first contacted about the job at eBay, and had already held a string of high-level jobs. A graduate of Princeton University and Harvard Business School, Whitman had in turn been a consultant in the San Francisco office of Bain & Company and a senior vice president of marketing for Disney Consumer Products. She left Disney in 1992 to work for the Stride Rite shoe company and eventually became president of its children's group. Ever on the move, she left that position in February 1995 to join Florists Transworld Delivery (FTD), Inc., the floral products company, as president and CEO. She moved on again to join toy maker Hasbro, Inc., as general manager of its preschool division, a position she held until March 1998.

Among other qualities, Whitman had something that eBay desperately needed: brand-building experience. With tens of thousands of sites appearing on the Web each year, eBay had to stand out above the clutter if it hoped to meet the growth goals everyone believed possible. Her consumer knowledge and marketing skills were also strong and coveted.

Whitman impressed Omidyar, Skoll, and Kagle as a strong and decisive executive, though not one with a need-to-dominate personality. This quality was consistent with eBay's existing culture—one that was open to the voices of customers and other employees. The ideal eBay executive, in their collective view, understood the importance of consensus, of listening, of giving employees a long leash, and of the company's "caring" environment. Whitman exhibited these characteristics, even though she was competitive and aggressive.

Whitman wasn't really looking for a new job when Benchmark partner David Beirne first contacted her.

When David asked if I would be interested in this new Internet company called eBay located in Silicon Valley, I frankly said, "not really." My husband was a neurosurgeon and ran the brain tumor program at Mass General [Hospital]. Our two boys were happy in school. I had made the transition to Hasbro just over a year before and things were going well there. I just couldn't see picking up and moving 3,000 miles across the country.[8]

Beirne persisted, and eventually got her to visit the company and its key people. As the head of a $600-million division, you have to wonder what her impressions were of Omidyar and Skoll—two 30-year-old guys working out of cramped rented offices with a few dozen mostly postadolescent employees. It was an engineering-driven operation in which practically no attention was paid to marketing. Would taking the job be a backward career step into the bush leagues?

Later, Whitman claimed to be struck by two things. First, unlike other online companies that were simply translating offline businesses into Internet-based analogs, this one had done something entirely different—something that could not have been done effectively offline. Second, she was impressed by the emotional connection between eBay users and the service.

Whitman found herself saying yes to the offer made by Kagle and Omidyar. In March 1998, she joined the company and moved to San Jose. Her family soon followed, and her husband joined the medical school of nearby Stanford University. She was given a $145,000 salary and qualified for a bonus of up to $100,000—roughly twice the annual compensation of Omidyar and Skoll. By the standards of big-league businesses, this was small potatoes. The big perk, of course, was an option to purchase 7.2 million shares of the company's stock (roughly a 6 percent stake) at $0.022 per share. The exercise of that option, and the eventual ascent of eBay shares in the open market, would make Meg Whitman a billionaire.

As an outsider brought in to run the operation, Whitman was naturally concerned about her role relative to that of the company founder. She knew that she couldn't do her job effectively if she was hamstrung by a controlling personality. Would Omidyar reserve all important decisions to himself? Would he undermine her effectiveness through a pattern of overruling her plans and directives? There were plenty of examples of this behavior in modern American business, and the vexing relationship between Apple founder Steve Jobs and his handpicked CEO, John Scully, was still fresh in the collective memory of the Valley. As it turned out, founder Omidyar was more than happy to leave the day-to-day details of the growing business to her. He was, after all, a concept guy, and he wanted to dedicate his attention to the company's strategic direction and its community of users.

Once she settled in, Whitman recognized the need for other voices at the top—outside board members who understood the challenges of expanding in new and unexplored business terrain, and who could provide advice and feedback. Kagle and his Benchmark partners knew lots of people like this, and helped the company recruit Howard Schultz, chairman and CEO of Starbucks, and Scott Cook, chairman of Intuit, as board members. Both men had created successful enterprises in previously undeveloped consumer markets.

➤ Building Infrastructure

Computing power is what makes an Internet auction feasible. More than in just about any other online activity, the union of digital information systems and a business concept has proven to be a marriage made in heaven, making it possible (by early 2000) for a few hundred people to handle transactions worth over $7 million every day of the year. This would not be possible without systems capable of real-time reporting on 4 million current auctions and even more competing bids.

Initially, eBay had developed proprietary software capable of supporting a robust, scalable user interface and transaction-processing system. Today, that system can handle all aspects of the auction process. It sends e-mails when users register for the service, when they place a successful bid, and when they are outbid, and it communicates the outcome of auctions in which they participate. The same system sends daily status updates to active sellers and bidders and maintains user registration information, account information, current auctions, and historical listings. All of this information is archived to a data warehouse.

Working around the clock (with weekly scheduled downtime for maintenance), the eBay system keeps track of every listing and every seller-selected enhancement option. When an auction successfully closes, the system automatically calculates the fee, bills the seller's billing account, and sends a monthly invoice via e-mail. Most invoices are billed directly to seller credit-card accounts.

Other parts of the eBay information infrastructure support eBay customer service and the various community bulletin boards and chat rooms that undergird the online user community.

The entire system includes company-owned and -operated equipment and other equipment provided by outside service providers. eBay's share of the total system consists of Sun database servers running Oracle relational database management systems and a suite of Internet servers that operate on Microsoft's Windows NT. Load-balancing systems and redundant servers provide for fault tolerance. System hardware is hosted in close proximity to the company's San Jose headquarters at the facilities of Exodus Communications and at AboveNet, where redundant communications lines and emergency power backup are maintained.

Since the company's inception, eBay managers have had to deal with two serious systems challenges: scaling up to meet exploding demand, and service outages. We'll get to both of these in later chapters.

➤ Beyond Start-up

Plans to go public with eBay were already afoot when Meg Whitman joined up in March 1998. Omidyar, chief financial officer Gary Bengier, and their Benchmark partners had already targeted the third quarter of that year as the time to launch the IPO.

Timing is everything in the IPO game. Every company hopes to bring its securities to market when investors are confident and eager to catch the next big wave. But the long period involved in floating securities makes hitting the right window of opportunity a guessing game. From the viewpoint of spring 1998, the omens were immensely favorable. The stock market had enjoyed tremendous strength, and the Dow Jones Industrial Average soared more than 1,000 points (13 percent) by midyear. Halfway through July, however, everyone's worst fear became a reality. Prices began to slip, and the market took a gut-wrenching dive of 18 percent by the end of September, just as Omidyar and associates were working with their investment bankers to offer their first public shares. Even the more important NASDAQ index hit the skids (see Figure 2.1). Meanwhile, CEO Whitman had been meeting with investors and securities dealers on a 10-day, 21-city road show.

Despite the storm clouds, the company completed its initial public offering on September 24, 1998, in a deal underwritten by Goldman Sachs, Donaldson, Lufkin & Jenrette (DLJ), Bancamerica Robertson Stephens, and BT Alex. Brown. It sold 4,025,000 shares for net proceeds of $66.1 million. At the same time, all outstanding shares of the company's convertible preferred and mandatorily redeemable preferred stock were converted into 27.8 million shares of common.

But what would eBay do with all of that money? Unlike almost all other dot-com companies, it was successfully financing most of its growth through positive cash flow. There was a $431,000 line of credit to be paid off, but that left some $65 million in spare change with no particular purpose other than as a war chest to fund future acquisitions and technology investments.

Investors who bought up eBay shares during the IPO were quickly in the money. During the first day of after-

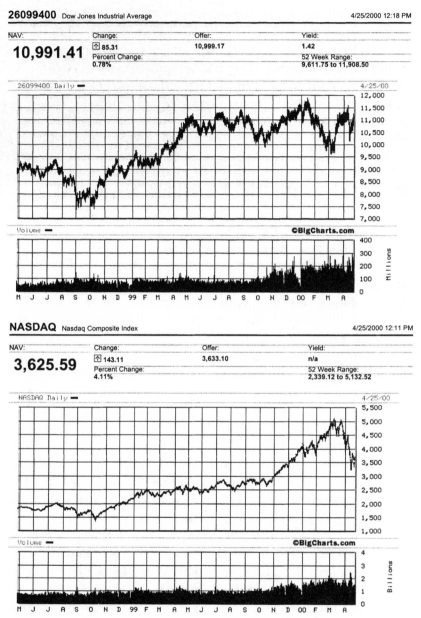

Figure 2.1 The Dow Jones Industrial Average and NASDAQ Composite Index. *(From www.bigcharts.com. Reproduced with permission.)*

market trading, share prices rose from $18 to $54, before settling back to $48 at the close. By year-end 1998, they would close at $80. And there was lots of price appreciation ahead for those who had the faith and fortitude to hold on. Six months after the IPO, share prices topped the $200 mark, and despite many ups and downs, reached $234 in late March 2000.

■ TWO KEY DECISIONS SPELLED SUCCESS

Looking back over the short course of the company's evolution, Mike Malone now believes that eBay's success is the outcome of two key decisions that, at the time they were made, could easily have gone a different way. "At the time, these seemed like unimportant decisions, and you could easily have justified making opposite choices. In fact, the opposite choices were even more justifiable." Those two decisions, in Malone's view, were (1) *to let anybody sell anything,* and (2) *to take a hands-off approach to user transactions.* Both decisions, per Malone, were motivated by the founders' instinctive trust in users, and both decisions— perhaps unwittingly—gave their business model infinite scale potential.

Opening the site to auctions of *anything* instantly eliminated whatever fences the business model could have built around the company's potential size. There would be no fences! "The big mistake made by the computer auction sites [which foreshadowed eBay] was that they narrowed themselves to a particular type of product," according to Malone. "Pierre and Jeff [in effect] said 'No, we're going to leave it wide open and let people sell anything they want.' " The result is that today, eBay is free to grow and expand into whatever product categories are available from sellers and valued by bidders. Like a big amoeba, the company has the flexibility to alter its shape and extend itself in the direction of new opportunities even as it draws away from categories of dwindling consumer interest. "eBay is an absolutely adaptive creature," says Malone.

The decision to take a hands-off approach to transactions between sellers and bidders helped the company avoid shackles that would have weighed it down as it grew. Auctioneers who took the traditional auction model onto the Internet brought along something they should have left behind: holding the goods and the money. "You cannot scale up that model," says Malone, citing Butterfield & Butterfield and Christie's, which he believes are about as big as they can become. "These can sell 2,000 items a week, but they can't scale up to a million."

As an eyewitness to these key decisions, Malone recollects that they were made very quickly and without a great deal of investigation or discussion. What drove them, in his opinion, were the trusting attitudes of Omidyar and Skoll toward their customers. "Everytime eBay has made a mistake, it has been because they tried to impose something top-down onto its users," he asserts, citing recent pricing changes, which caused near-mutiny among users. "And every time it has trusted users to decide what needed to be done, it has been successful."

■ THE REWARDS OF ENTREPRENEURSHIP

As founder, Pierre Omidyar received 44.1 million common shares of the corporation. He exchanged some 30 percent of these shares for the company's entire issue of Series A preferred stock, which was issued in December 1996 in a recapitalization. Those preferred shares were automatically converted back to common shares when the corporation made its first public offering in September 1998.

In the wake of the IPO and the rising stock value that followed, Omidyar's stake was worth over $4 billion. What does a guy do with all that wealth? Not much, apparently. Even a year after the IPO, Omidyar was reportedly still driving the same Volkswagen Jetta he had owned for years, and living in the same rented house. He has since moved on to Paris.

Jeff Skoll likewise shared in the bounty. His participation in the founding of the company earned him roughly 22.8 million shares of eBay common stock. These made him, at age 32, a billionaire three times over. Like his friend and associate, however, money doesn't appear to have influenced Skoll's habits. He held onto the 10-year-old Mazda he owned before his sudden wealth, and for some time continued living in a rented house with five roommates. "I never cared much about money," Skoll told a reporter. "It's pretty ironic, isn't it?"[9]

Benchmark really hit the jackpot with eBay. Its $5 million investment produced such a prodigious return that the computer on which it made its rate-of-return calculations froze. Whoever entered the formula had not been thinking on a grand enough scale, and failed to provide enough digit spaces to calculate Benchmark's 49,000 percent return. This trumped all previous venture capital returns in the collective memory of the industry, including those of Microsoft, Cisco, Sun, and other big successes, and gave Benchmark major-league bragging rights.

To their credit, eBay's newly minted millionaires were quick to give away portions of their sudden wealth. In June 1998 the company established the eBay Foundation, funding it initially with 321,750 shares of eBay stock. Community Foundation of Silicon Valley (CFSV), a tax-exempt public charity whose mission is to promote philanthropy and build a strong community, was engaged to manage the fund. Later, Omidyar and his wife Pam donated 15,000 additional shares to the fund (and another 50,000 shares to CFSV). Jeff Skoll was also an active contributor. More significant was Pierre and Pam Omidyar's pledge to give away all but 1 percent of their net worth over a 25-year period.

■ "WE ARE A COMMUNITY"

eBay's success by early 1999 was both substantial and remarkably sudden. Few business enterprises have come so far so fast with so few assets and so few employees. Pierre Omidyar's concept of person-to-person auction trading and the mechanisms for making it efficient and fun facilitated that success. But these would have counted for little if millions of individuals and small businesses had not forged a community of interest around the company's site—a community bonded through mutual trust, standards of fair dealing, and a sense of ownership of the site itself. Few corporations have enjoyed such a privileged relationship with their customers. It is the part of the "eBay phenomenon" to which we turn next.

Chapter

The eBay Nation

Like a Middle Eastern bazaar, eBay has attracted a diverse community of active traders. Most are buyers and sellers who enter the site infrequently to unload a piece of unused merchandise or, conversely, to acquire the same—hopefully at a bargain price. Others are serious collectors and dealers of books, antiques, coins, automobiles, and other items for whom online auctions have vastly expanded the pool of available items and trading partners.

Still others have turned their hobbies into viable home businesses, affording them opportunities to earn livelihoods and to more effectively balance work and home life. Larry (aka wishmaker) falls into this group. Larry is a 40-year-old father of three living in Springfield, Oregon. Disabled with spinal arthritis, but too proud and ambitious not to work, he found auction selling something that he could do well and has turned it into a credible means of support for his family.

In March 1998, Larry and his wife began selling his gold-issue stamps on the site, and found that they could not keep up with demand. "When I realized that there was a viable market on eBay, I began contacting wholesalers [to acquire more product], and I've been selling doll-house miniatures and similar things ever since."

Like thousands of other sole proprietors, Larry has created a profitable business, using his home as an operations center and eBay as his principal distribution channel. According to his own estimate, he is now running between 100 and 200 auctions each week. "During eBay's free listing day I listed 443 items—and I sold about 300." These auctions keep Larry scrambling seven days per week. Acquiring merchandise and posting it to the site with graphics and complete descriptions, answering e-mail inquiries from bidders, contacting winning bidders, packing and mailing, collecting and processing checks, posting feedback on buyers—it takes up most of his time. Still, he makes time in his schedule to share his experience with other eBayers who are trying to use the site more effectively.

Through 1999, Larry experienced a number of ups and downs in his business—many of which he attributes to eBay: site crashes, pages not loading, system slowdowns, tardy end-of-auction notices, and policy changes. "If eBay has a glitch in its system, it affects every buyer and seller," he says. Nevertheless, he sees these problems as inevitable snafus in a new way of doing business, and he anticipates better things in the future. "The online business is going to take off. This year [2000] should be a very profitable one for anyone doing business on the Internet, especially on auction sites."

From a strictly business viewpoint, the most interesting members of eBay's online community are people like Larry: the dealers and other small-business operators who are learning to use the site as a new and profitable channel of distribution. eBay has expanded their geographic reach, added tremendous depth to their pools of potential buyers, and made it all happen at remarkably low cost. Today, these site users account for the bulk of eBay's gross revenues.

■ EBAYSIAN COMMUNITY AND CULTURE

The company makes much in its promotional literature about its "community of users" and how it is held together by equality, empowerment, and bonds of trust, mutual respect, and responsibility between buyers and sellers. Many users share this view. As an eBayer from western Michigan stated on his About Me page: "eBay is a community, and just like any town, village or city, it takes nice caring people to make it a good place to be. I treat eBay as if it were my own, because it is, just like it is yours. You and I have the power to make it a better place or just another on-line auction house."

Meg Whitman likes to say that eBay is putting old-fashioned person-to-person relationships back into American business—an online analog to the face-to-face transactions that most people experience in traditional commerce:

> If you think back a hundred years, we were all individual proprietors who cared a lot about the merchandise we sold. You had a connection with [the community]. As retail evolved, that kind of went away. eBay [has brought] Main Street back into the economy and enabled small dealers and individuals to sell the merchandise they love. [This] allows you to have an incredibly personal shopping experience as opposed to walking into these superstores where you're lucky if you can find someone. They certainly don't know about the merchandise, nor do they love that merchandise. [They] cannot answer the second- and third-order questions. Virtually all of our sellers are small proprietors who give you a very customized and knowledgeable experience.[1]

The integrity of the site depends, in fact, on this sentiment of commercial communitarianism, on people's honesty and natural sense of fair play, on their active acceptance of auction rules and procedures, and on their vigilance in spotting and reporting online misbehaviors. As a Wall Street watcher of the company once noted, "The three most important keys of [eBay's] success [are] community, community, community."[2]

Most credit founder Pierre Omidyar with the unique eBay culture, which, as he once told interviewers from Harvard Business School, is based on "a respect for our community."

> eBay wouldn't exist if it wasn't for our community. . . . At eBay, our customer experience is based on how our customers deal with our other customers. They rarely deal directly with the company. So how do you control the customer to customer experience? We can't control how one person treats another. . . . The only thing we can do is to influence customer behavior by encouraging them to adopt certain values. And those values are to assume that people are basically good, to give people the benefit of the doubt, and to treat people with respect.[3]

Nice sentiments and wishful thinking, however, do not create lasting communities. John Perry Barlow, cofounder of the Electronic Frontier Foundation, made the point in our interview that "community doesn't do well on the basis of good intentions," citing the many utopian societies that have come and gone over the centuries. Good intentions must be supplemented with the bonding power of institutions and mechanisms of social intercourse. These provide a structural framework around which real and sustainable community can be created. Either by design or accident, eBay has provided framework elements of specific services and features: bulletin boards, feedback ratings, customer support, and the system's main chat room, the eBay Café.

➤ Voices of Discontent

Not everyone is happy in the eBay nation. Like any community, there's a certain amount of discontent. Just go to one of the chat or discussion boards and you'll get an eyeful. Consider this exchange between users A and B:

> **A:** I am getting sick of ebay's Gestapo like attitude towards its site and customers. Now eBay is telling me what my auction must look like and sending me threats of cancellation of my auctions and/or suspension from eBay. A 700 rating and $500 per month to eBay . . . and they could care less!

> **B:** Consider yourself lucky however sick that may sound! Another seller came up here recently who had ALL 66 AUCTIONS CANCELLED WITHOUT WARNING . . . Yes, welcome to the new and improved eBay New World Order, where 85% of us are so happy with eBay customer service!!!

> **A:** I WILL NOT list with eBay ever again for the same reasons you stated. They have done NOTHING for the sellers who continuously make them over $400 to $500 a month. They sent me a SMALL t-shirt when I specifically asked for an xtra large and had the nerve to ask me to send it back (at my expense) and they would send me the correct size!! I threw the damn thing in the trash!!

Or this angry user's comments:

> **C:** Ah, now eBay bans lookalike guns. Are you trying to create a utopian environment for us? Oh wait, I know what it is—that liberal bay area element is infecting your business. Sad, very very sad.

It's impossible to measure how deep the warm and fuzzy eBay community spirit actually goes. Participants interviewed for this book exhibited a range of feelings on this issue. It is even more difficult to correlate community spirit with eBay's operating results, though it's easy to believe in a positive relationship between the two.

Even if we assume a *modest* sense of community spirit among eBay users, that spirit sets it apart from nearly all U.S. corporations—both online and off. Dell and Hewlett-Packard make great equipment, and their customers are generally pretty happy with it, but they feel no sense of community with these companies or their fellow users. They may communicate with the manufacturers through customer feedback questionnaires, but they don't chat—not with the companies, and not with other customers. Even on the Internet, it's hard to find company sites that exhibit any characteristics of active community, iVillage being a notable exception. The reason is surely tied to the fact that users of these sites deal directly with the sponsoring enterprise and *not* with each other.

➤ Small Dealers Go Online

eBay was created as a person-to-person channel of exchange, but that initial vision is now overshadowed by small-business-to-consumer transactions. Today an estimated 80 percent of eBay's revenues are generated by only 20 percent of its registered users—mostly small businesses that use the site and competing portals as their public storefronts. Barr's Fiddle Shop in Galax, Virginia, provides a good example.

Tom Barr first began acquiring, reconditioning, and selling fiddles and other traditional musical instruments in the 1950s. Galax and its environs was then, and continues to be, a vibrant center of old-time and bluegrass music, a part of America where vintage fiddles, mandolins, banjos, and guitars are fairly common household items. He first operated this business out of his home, but as it grew, opened a small retail store in town.

Barr developed a reputation for high-quality instruments and gradually acquired a clientele of musicians and collectors, mostly within a 100- to 200-mile radius of Galax. Those who understand stringed instrument players know their appetites. Many guitar players, for example, suffer from a chronic condition known as GAS, or guitar acquisition syndrome. Two or three guitars are insufficient, and they are always alert to a special instrument. Fiddle players are highly susceptible to a similar condition. Most own several instruments, if only to avoid the chore of retuning between different musical pieces.

Despite regular traffic in stringed instruments in the Galax area, Barr's Fiddle Shop—like many small retailers—found itself on a revenue plateau. There was only so much business to be had. And that business was markedly seasonal. October, November, and December were dependably big months, but sales dropped off dramatically in January, February, and March.

Then came eBay.

"What got us started," says Tom's son, Steve, "was a friend of ours, who began experimenting with it. He didn't have a business of his own, but he was interested in photography and began taking pictures of his instruments and putting them on eBay. And he did really well."

The Barrs quickly saw the auction site as an opportunity for business expansion. Steve, who enjoys photography, soon learned how to create excellent images of his instruments, scan them, and get them onto the site. In January 1999, Steve began posting selected instruments on eBay. The results were surprising. Using online auctions to supplement their regular retail store sales, the Barrs transformed their three lowest revenue months into their three *highest* sales producers—*doubling* the level of sales produced in October, November, and December. "We sold everything we put on there," says Steve, often at much higher prices than they would have commanded in the store.

The reason for the sales increase was straightforward: The Barrs had expanded their geographic reach. "Before eBay, we had about one thousand regular customers who would come in every year," says Steve Barr, and another 500 or so random visitors. Most of the regulars lived within 200 miles of Galax. eBay expanded this clientele many-fold, bringing in buyers from all over the United States and around the world. Many of these, particularly those living in the southeastern United States, have since become regular retail clients, stopping in Barr's Fiddle Shop whenever their travels bring them near the south-western corner of Virginia.

The Barrs also experienced two other benefits from online sales: rapid inventory turnover and improved margins. Their regular retail inventory often sits in a display case for months until a committed buyer happens by. "During that time, you run the risk of someone dropping it, busting it up, and it's sitting here for three or four months." In contrast, most of the Barrs' auction transactions are consummated in three to seven days. This rapid turnover has reduced the small company's working capital requirements.

Profit margins on the Barr's auctioned items are almost always higher than those associated with retail sales. In one case, furious bidding by eager collectors drove the final bid on one classic fiddle to more than *twice* the price that the Barrs would have placed on the instrument had it been offered in their retail store. What accounts for this behavior on the part of online bidders? John Parkinson, an e-commerce consultant with Ernst & Young LLP, observes that "collectors in particular do not exhibit rational price behavior." They have no price expectations, in his view, and are more inclined to bid "what they can afford" than bid up to a rationally determined point of value.[4] This is not the behavior of professional collectors, who are knowledgeable about valuations and much more calculating in the levels to which they will bid. But amateur collectors are more numerous, and by all appearances are more driven by their desires than by trained value calculators. A case in point is one Galax resident who heard that her late brother's handmade mandolin was being offered on an eBay auction. Being unacquainted with the online world, she rushed down to Barr's Fiddle Shop to discuss the situation with Tom and Steve. They showed her how to access the site, how to become a registered user, and how to bid for her brother's instrument. "Another guy also wanted that mandolin," Steve explained, "and the two of them went back and forth until the mandolin went for about fifteen hundred dollars, when a reasonable price would have been seven hundred to eight hundred dollars."

Increased unit sales, higher margins, and more rapid inventory turnover—these three factors are raising the performance of Barr's Fiddle Shop and the thousands of other small businesses that have learned how to successfully engage in online auctions. One critical constraint, however, imposes a natural ceiling on their use of this new and profitable channel: product availability. When the Barrs first listed online, they began with an inventory of 20 instruments, but this was quickly depleted. "We ran out of stuff," says Steve Barr. Since the supply of vintage instruments does not expand with demand, success with online distribution has forced them to be more active in acquiring instruments, both locally and through a geographically distributed set of contacts. Even so, by late 1999 they could support auctions of only two to three collector-quality instruments per month. But since these sell in three to seven days, they aren't complaining. (The supply of quality collectible products was cited by other sellers interviewed as a limiting factor in running an online auction business.)

➤ Nonauction Transactions

Many eBay auctions are never consummated—at least not through the auction site. This happens when bidders fail to reach the *reserve price* stipulated by sellers. Under eBay's rules, sellers have the right to hold a reserve-price auction, one in which they can set a dollar amount (the reserve price) below which they are not obliged to sell the listed item. The reserve price is known to eBay and to the seller, but not to the bidding public.[5]

ADVICE FOR SELLERS

Every seller wants to get the highest possible price when selling an item via online auction. Successful sellers agree that the best way to do this is to provide excellent photographs and complete descriptions. "You want an in-depth written description," advises Steve Barr, "and your pictures should show every detail. That way the buyer will know exactly what he's bidding for, and will likely bid more." Bookseller Shirley Bryant (aka aaabooks) concurs. She has a return policy that allows winning bidders to return books that are not as described. And since she hates getting them back, she overdescribes her items, down to the tiniest wrinkle on the dust jacket. Her practice is to spell out absolutely everything so that people know exactly what they are getting. "My philosophy," she says "is to tell all the bad things—and then I tell all the good things. If I'm selling something really expensive, I put up three [photo] scans . . . so that people see exactly what they're getting."

Their advice conforms with financial theory. Uncertainty about the features and conditions of an item represents risk to the buyer, who naturally holds back on his or her bidding to compensate for the perceived risk.

Successful sellers also point to full and complete disclosure as their best insurance against returns, complaints, and a negative seller rating in eBay's Feedback Forum. If there's a blemish on the finish of a violin, or a tear on the dust jacket of a first-edition book, for example, these defects should be disclosed to potential buyers.

Other successful sellers advise users to keep their auction listings uncluttered. Kathleen (aka kleodnile) tells seller to avoid loading up their listings with extraneous pictures and music that are slow to download for most users.

Sellers pay an *insertion fee* based on either the minimum bidding price or the reserve price. If bidding fails to reach or exceed the reserve price, the seller is not obliged to complete a transaction with the highest bidder, and the auction goes unconsummated. eBay keeps the insertion fee in these cases but loses out on the *final value fee,* which the seller is obliged to pay *only* if a deal is made online.[6] And that final value fee is the larger of the two fees.

Consider a dealer who lists a rare coin with a reserve price of $400. She may have chosen that price because it represents her investment in the coin plus a small profit, or because she believes that she can sell the coin in her retail store for that amount. By setting the reserve price at $400, she avoids the risk of losing money on the transaction, even as she preserves her upside potential. Someone, for example, might pay $700 or $800 for this coin in order to complete a collection. Because the reserve-price feature works in favor of sellers exclusively, many buyers will not participate in reserve auctions. They figure that the reserve effectively eliminates any chance of getting a significant bargain—*their* upside. And they are probably right in many cases.

But the failure of buyers to reach a seller's reserve price does not mean that a transaction will not take place. Sellers interviewed for this book reported a lively *offline* commerce between themselves and unsuccessful bidders. One dealer cited his practice of sending e-mails to each of the three highest bidders, stating "Our reserve price was not met in the recent auction. However, if you would like to purchase the item, we are agreeable to selling it to you for $_____." This dealer reports that many of these queries turn into direct sales. Another dealer reported using a similar approach, but follows a policy of offering the item at the reserve price plus shipping, *less* the final value fee that would otherwise have been paid to eBay ($25.63 on a $1,000 item). The bean counters at eBay must hate this practice, but it is a fact of life in online auction commerce. One dealer reported that 50 to 60 percent of his revenues came from off-auction transactions like those described here.

➤ Solutions for High-Volume Sellers

eBay and similar sites were designed for the needs of casual users, and they work fine for them. However, the growing numbers of high-volume sellers—people who auction 200 or more items per week—face daunting back-office chores that effectively limit their potential revenues and profits. The time involved in listing each item to an auction site can be laborious and time-consuming, sometimes requiring an hour per item. Photographs and descriptions must be posted. Each auction must be monitored, and questions from bidders must be answered. Once an auction has been completed, sellers are obliged to notify winning bidders via e-mail of their success, indicate the price (including shipping), process incoming checks, pack and ship items, and send follow-up e-mails. Conscientious sellers always provide a feedback rating on the buyer. Together, these chores require substantial hours of work. And because the time involved in handling an average eBay transaction ($47) is roughly the same as for one involving a $1,000 rare coin, many volume sellers of low-priced items must find themselves working for very low hourly wages.

These back-office impediments, and the growing number of volume sellers, have stimulated the development of specialized software and independent auction service businesses that aim to improve seller productivity. The first of these are image-hosting services. Every seller who wants to embellish an offering with a photograph must find a place on the Internet to store that image. Some users receive limited free space for this purpose from their Internet service providers. Others must turn to other sources, such as Photopoint.com, AuctionWatch.com, and Pongo.com. Some provide free space, while others charge a small fee for every image.

A number of software tools have also been developed to overcome the productivity problem. eBay provides a free bulk-selling tool, Mister Lister, which has gone through a number of refinements. Others have been developed by third parties. In November 1999, Andale, Inc., a Santa Clara firm, went online with what it describes as a total solution for volume auction sellers: a Web-based auction business management service. According to Andale's cofounder and CEO, Munjal Shah, the service aims to deliver the industry's first resource "for automating and managing all aspects of selling—from product merchandising to financial management, sales automation, customer communications, supplier sourcing and other back office services."[7] Like eBay, Andale makes money by taking a small fraction from every transaction.

■ WHOM DO YOU TRUST?

Every merchant must build a foundation of trust between his or her business and its customers, and the eBay community of buyers, sellers, and site operator is no different. Customers must believe that their purchases represent good value, that they are what they were represented to be, that they will perform as expected, and that the vendors will stand behind what they sell. "People won't conduct transactions with each other unless they have trusting relationships first," according to founder Omidyar. "That trusting relationship will only occur if they treat each other well. So there is a direct correlation between how our customers treat each other and the performance of our business."[8]

Trust appears not to be a problem for Amazon, Garden .com, PC Warehouse, Staples.com, and the hundreds of other e-tailers with whom people have grown accustomed to doing online business every day. Do you have any trepidation about ordering a new book through Amazon? Are you afraid that Staples will stiff you on a box of computer paper? Would you have second thoughts about purchasing a self-configured PC from Gateway or Dell? Probably not. Ordering from one of these companies requires no more trust than ordering from a direct-mail catalog. Customers recognize them as legitimate operators who stand behind their merchandise. The merchandise, in any case, is fairly standard, and price comparisons can be made at different sites—including brick-and-mortar retail stores.

An auction on eBay is much different. You may have total confidence in eBay, but as a bidder or seller, you're not dealing with a brand-name company but with a cyber-stranger. eBay makes no warranty about the object you're bidding for. It simply provides a venue in which you and another party can do business. As its user agreement states:

> Our site acts as the venue for sellers to list items (or, as appropriate, solicit offers to buy) and buyers to bid on items. We are not involved in the actual transaction between buyers and sellers. As a result, we have no control over the quality, safety or legality of the items advertised, the truth or accuracy of the listings, the ability of sellers to sell items or the ability of buyers to buy items. We cannot ensure that a buyer or seller will actually complete a transaction. . . .
>
> Because we are not involved in the actual transaction between buyers and sellers, in the event that you have a dispute with one or more users, you release eBay (and our officers, directors, agents, subsidiaries and employees) from claims, demands, damages. . . .
>
> We do not control the information provided by other users which is made available through our system. You may find other user's information to be offensive, harmful, inaccurate, or deceptive. . . .[9]

This language doesn't exactly encourage you to join in the fun.

Every business transaction is based on a greater or lesser degree of trust, and online auction purchases must surely be on the *greater* end of the spectrum. When you see a baseball being auctioned for $3,800 because the seller purports that it was signed by the 1939 New York Yankees team, which included Joe DiMaggio, are you willing to trust that the signatures are genuine? How much trust would you need before you'd enter the bidding for a 1973 Ferrari at $85,000? How credible is the seller and his or her claim about the product's authenticity?

The company's literature claims that its site "was founded on the belief that most people are trustworthy and committed to honorable dealings with each other." A nice sentiment, but would you bet cash on it? Millions of users have. eBay users have demonstrated a remarkable degree of trust in people they've never met and in their claims that everything from Beanie Babies to paintings, automobiles, and thousands of other types of goods are what they purport to be.

eBay recognized the critical importance of trust between auction participants and has developed programs aimed at shoring up the natural sense of trustworthiness that it assumes animates its user community. These programs are designed to increase the user's comfort level in dealing with unknown trading partners in cyberspace.

"We are not encouraging blind trust," says Meg Whitman. "We are encouraging our community to think that basically 99 percent of the people out there are doing the right thing. If you assume that people are trying to do the right thing, you'll get through misunderstandings much easier, and it [will] be more fun and more pleasing to be in the community."[10]

➤ Hands On or Hands Off

As eBay grows larger and more popular, it is experiencing greater pressure—from buyers, consumer groups, lawsuits, and trade groups whose intellectual property rights are often infringed on auction sites—to take greater responsibility for transactions on its site. Rival Amazon Auctions is already doing so.

Taking greater responsibility for site transactions represents a trade-off for the company. On the positive side, it would enhance its image and reputation as a safe place to trade. The downside, according to Jupiter Communications analyst Michael May, is that "it would reduce their ability to scale and violate the purity of their [business] model." It's hard to see how anything less than a small army of employee-sleuths could effectively monitor the site's millions of auction listings, and guaranteeing offered items would both be costly and suck company personnel into endless disputes.

➤ The Feedback Forum

The Feedback Forum is eBay's most powerful mechanism for raising levels of trust and confidence among users. The forum encourages users to register their comments about other users (both buyers and sellers) with whom they have conducted transactions. More important, the company provides a positive-neutral-negative rating format that is both public and cumulative. Thanks to this forum, participants can build public reputations, just as traditional merchants and customers have always done in their communities. According to Shirley "aaabooks" Bryant, the rare-book seller from Oklahoma, "Feedback is the greatest thing that's happened to selling online."

Figure 3.1 presents feedback on a seller with the online user name f50gt as of 15 January 2000 (the comment list is abbreviated to save space). In reality, this seller is Nigel Carroll, a classic car dealer. (Note that the identities of the commenting users are concealed to protect their confidentiality.)

At the time he was interviewed for this book, Nigel's profile—which any potential bidder can check—showed that 16 comments had been made about him over the previous

User: xxxxxxx **Date:** 01/13/00, 08:00:49 PST
Praise: Easy, professional, no bs. Takes all the scare out of buying on line. Honestly!

User: xxxxxxx **Date:** 12/21/99, 14:23:54 PST
Praise: Item is awesome, excellent value and great transaction AAAAAAAA+++++++++++

User: xxxxxxx **Date:** 12/07/99, 20:31:31 PST
Praise: very positive, helpful and honest. vehicle was as presented. an easy transaction

User: xxxxxxx **Date:** 12/06/99, 18:02:00 PST
Praise: Nigel is very helpful, friendly, willing to go the extra mile, even post sale AAA++

User: xxxxxxx **Date:** 11/03/99, 05:37:42 PST
Praise: HONEST! FAST! HELPFUL! IT WAS GREAT TO DO BUSINESS WITH HIM! A+++

User: xxxxxxx **Date:** 10/08/99, 16:09:46 PDT
Praise: Excellent communication, very professional, would do business with again. A++!

User: xxxxxxx **Date:** 10/02/99, 16:30:17 PDT
Praise: Nigel is an excellent seller! He was so kind, honest and professional!!!!!!!!!!!

User: xxxxxxx **Date:** 10/01/99, 19:15:38 PDT
Praise: VERY HAPPY WITH CAR . . . GREAT COMMU-NICATION. . . . THANKS RICHARD & NIGEL . . . I LOVE IT!

User: xxxxxxx **Date:** 09/30/99, 22:01:28 PDT
Praise: Smooth transaction. Car was just as described. VERY HAPPY. Highly recommend. A++

Figure 3.1 Feedback on Nigel Carroll. *(From eBay, with permission from Nigel Carroll.)*

six months. It also indicated the number of positive, neutral, and negative comments (all were positive in this case).

When users have developed a positive reputation, eBay places stars next to their user names. Stars are color-coded to indicate the volume of feedback received.

For regular sellers, the trust generated through a high feedback rating is an absolute must for doing business in cyberspace. Wary bidders look to see several things:

- How many auctions the seller has transacted
- How previous buyers have rated their experience with the seller
- Verbal comments about the seller

A positive feedback rating and glowing verbal comments from past buyers are a bidder's greatest assurance that a seller is a person with whom they can do business with confidence. Knowing this, sellers generally work very hard to establish and maintain highly positive ratings.

Buyers also accumulate feedback ratings, and sellers can use these to screen out unreliable trading partners—for example, people who make a winning bid but fail to follow through with payment. Sellers should not read too much into a buyer's feedback rating, however, without digging a little deeper. Nigel Carroll explains why:

> A woman recently purchased a 500SEL from me, and she had about seventeen positive feedbacks—about as many as me at the time. I thought "This looks like a good buyer." And she was.
>
> She called me at the end of the auction to say that she'd fly in the next day to pick up the car, which she did. She came with cash—about $4,000—looked at the car for about twenty minutes, got in, and drove it back to Sacramento. When I went back to her feedback file I discovered that none of her previous purchases had been for more than $5.99!

➤ About Me

Ratings are very useful, but many of us feel better about bidding online if we know something about the seller. Does she seem fair and businesslike? Is he a seasoned dealer, or a rank amateur? eBay makes it possible for every registered user to describe him- or herself and even leave a photographic image. For example, here's Nigel Carroll's About Me information:

Hi, my name is Nigel Carroll
WELCOME TO MY SALE!

I hope that the information on this page will help you to decide to bid on my item. You are probably looking at a motor vehicle, and considering bidding for it. Before you do, please read on.

BUYING A CAR ON THE INTERNET

Buying anything on the Internet without seeing it can be a little scary, so I will attempt to put your mind at rest! I have been a collector, buyer, and seller of motor vehicles for thirty-three years. It started as a hobby and became a business. My company is called INTERNATIONAL CLASSIC CARS INC. My associate Richard Mitchell and I have over fifty years of combined experience in the classic car market place, both in the United States and in Europe. ICC is licensed and bonded in the State of California. We specialize in providing motor vehicles to the film industry for use in commercials, music videos, and movies. Occasionally we have vehicles for sale, either purchased by us or consigned to ICC by the owner for sale on his or her behalf.

Based in Los Angeles, California, the vast majority of our vehicles have spent their entire motoring lives in our sunny dry climate. In 1999 ICC offered close to thirty classic cars for sale on eBay, most of them sold first time out, others took a little longer, but so far I have had no complaints and I am grateful to those customers who left me feedback, which speaks for itself. Our cars have been shipped as far away as Europe, and have been collected by customers who have flown into Los Angeles from all over the United States to drive their purchases home. Our listings on eBay include a Volkswagen Bug, which sold at $1,600 all the way up to a Ferrari Testarossa with a high bid of $53,500.00. Our goal is to offer quality cars at a price that is generally lower than you will find in your local paper.

We will be more than happy to answer as many questions as possible, and send more photographs to you via e-mail. If you are the successful high bidder we will send you a video of the vehicle if requested so you will get a better idea of the condition of your purchase prior to making your travel arrangements to pick it up. We urge you to ask questions BEFORE bidding, and please don't bid if you do not have the funds available at the auction close to complete the purchase. We have added a link below to Kelley Blue Book Used Car Values for your convenience. We also buy classic cars. If you have a vehicle that you think might be of interest to us, for sale or use in a commercial, e-mail details. We can also help you find what you are looking for. WE ARE NOT SALESMEN, REMEMBER YOU SET THE PRICE! GOOD LUCK WITH YOUR BID! Thank you for visiting my page.*

*Source: Nigel Carroll, About Me page. Used with permission.

About Me pages like Nigel Carroll's give all sellers an opportunity to introduce themselves to potential customers, and to make a case for their background, experience, and professionalism. This information is a useful proxy for the face-to-face interactions that build trust in traditional venues of commerce.

Carroll, who operates his business in Los Angeles, confesses his initial surprise that anyone would buy his products over the Internet—people have substantial reservations about used vehicles that they can see, examine, and test drive before making an offer. He began listing on eBay in July 1999 at the suggestion of a friend. "I said 'you must be joking.' A used car has many things that can go wrong. It's hard enough to sell a used car to someone when he's looking at it."

The first car he listed was a 1972 350SL Mercedes, a two-seat sports car. "I was amazed," he recalls. "Within the first three days I had over thirty-seven e-mails." And this was before he had learned how to attach photos to his listings. Months later, when he had three Porsches simultaneously listed, his site counter registered a total of 17,000 hits within seven days.

Buyers far from Nigel Carroll's lot bid on his cars, and winners often travel from Seattle, Texas, and other out-of-state locations to pick them up. "The attraction of rust-free California cars," he says. Although he has shipped cars to England, the furthest drive-away buyer was from Dearborn, Michigan, who, with his wife, flew into Los Angeles airport, where Nigel picked them up. "It was already ten o'clock and dark here in LA. The car, which was bright red, looked brown under the sodium-iodine lights where it was parked. He saw the car and said 'This is beautiful, it's wonderful.' I asked him if he'd like to take a test ride, but he said 'I don't have time. I have to be back in Dearborn in three days.' We did the paperwork and off they went. Three days later he sent me an e-mail saying 'Thanks very much. It ran fine.' "

➤ SafeHarbor

SafeHarbor is not a program so much as it is a set of programs designed to ensure fair trading in the system and to solidify user confidence. It includes:

- A mechanism for reporting suspicious activities, such as any apparent manipulation of an auction or misrepresentations by bidders or sellers. eBay warns or suspends registered users who misuse the service or violate its terms.

- Information on banned auction items. eBay's policies, for example, forbid the auctioning of firearms, alcohol, adult materials, and other goods categories.
- Antipiracy and anti-infringement programs.
- A free program with Lloyds of London that insures every eligible transaction up to $200 (less a $25 deductible) in cases of actual fraud.
- A third-party escrow holder.

Each of these programs is designed to buttress the confidence of auction participants, and the last deserves special mention. eBay has worked out an arrangement in which a third-party provider, iEscrow, acts as escrow holder when parties agree to this arrangement. There are plenty of cases in which doing so makes sense for one or both parties. Suppose you had placed the winning bid for a very expensive rare coin. Normally, the seller would not ship the coin until you had provided payment, but you insist on seeing the coin and verifying its authenticity first. That's fine with the seller, but he needs some assurance that he'll either get the money or have his coin returned. After all, he doesn't know you any better than you know him. Here, an escrow arrangement solves the concerns of both buyer and seller. You send the money to the escrow holder, who notifies the seller that he can now ship the coin to you. Once you have ascertained its genuine character, you instruct the escrow holder to release the funds to the seller, and the deal is complete.

➤ Complaints and Fraud

Millions of annual transactions on the eBay site produce remarkably few complaints from users. According to company data, complaints number roughly 200 per million transactions (0.02 percent). Users resolve most of these complaints among themselves. Official cases of fraud are even more rare, at roughly 30 per million transactions (0.003 percent).

However, as the number of auctions increases, problem transactions are bound to increase. The company's stated goal is to reduce the absolute number of problem transactions. To that end, it works with law enforcement and its content owners to identify and ferret out illegal and infringing items and fraud.

For Internet auction sites in general, the major area of complaint involves misrepresentation by sellers. Misrepresentation can take many forms: misleading descriptions, the deliberate omission of flaws and defects, manipulated photos of items for sale, and the like.

The low rate of fraud recorded by the company begs the question: How many cases go *unreported?* And what about unethical behaviors undetected or unreported by users: deadbeat bidding, shill bidding, and item misrepresentation? The National Consumer League (NCL), the largest U.S. nonprofit consumer action group, found that online auctions as a group generated five times as many consumer complaints as other online commerce sites.[11] Its Internet Fraud Watch unit compiles reports of fraud into a database it shares with law enforcement groups. Eightyseven percent of cases of online fraud reported to this unit involved online auctions.

Not one of the trust-building elements just described can provide a foolproof trading environment. For example, in November 1999 a California man was sentenced to 14 months in prison and fined $100,000 in connection with a number of charges, which included defrauding eBay customers by never shipping items for which they had paid. Even the Feedback Forum is not a solid filter of unscrupulous operators, as one *New York Times* reader asserted in a letter to the editor: "I have found that the ratings given to people on a site can be misleading. All a person needs to do if he or she gets bad ratings on an Internet auction or swap site is to sign on as a different member and continue to cheat other members. It cost me $493 to find that out."[12]

Cases like this notwithstanding, the various mechanisms put in place by the company appear to provide the assurance that eBay users can conduct business with confidence. (See Chapter 8 for a discussion of the sale of illegal and counterfeit items on eBay and other auction sites.)

■ THE EBAY CAFÉ

The Café chat room is one of the cornerstones of eBay's community-building effort. It is the online analog of the traditional small-town coffee shop where people stop to relax, catch up on news and hearsay, and exchange information. For example, eBay's Café posts a daily mix of remarks, user tips, sociable banter, and even advice for the lovelorn—whatever people have on their minds.

> Here are the pictures of my cats.
>
> · · · ·
>
> Fred, I'm working on my web page now. Could you look at it and give me some suggestions. It's starting to look good, but I want it to be eye catching and fun.
>
> · · · ·
>
> Love must be based on mutual friendship, respect and trust, Bill. An internet relationship can start the ball rolling, but you have to spend time together.
>
> · · · ·
>
> Internet romances are okay with me, too, but true commitment is when you're sick and your old man is patting your back while your heads in the toilet.
>
> · · · ·
>
> My squirrels are feasting on some old hush puppies I found in the back of the frig. You would think it was candy. They love french fries too!

. . . .

I think I'm falling in love with you.

. . . .

Gotta go! Time to do the laundry and start the dinner.

Discount the useful technical advice from the eBay Café and what remains is mostly social chatter—not unlike the banter exchanged in traditional shops and offices. This appears to serve the same need for social connectivity. The Café brings thousands of people back to the site every day, and many carry their connections outside the walls of the Café, communicating directly with each other through e-mails, personal phone calls, and face-to-face visits.

"I have met some of the most interesting people at the Café," says Kathleen (aka kleodnile) from Duluth, Minnesota, who makes and sells stained glass as a hobby and part-time business. "They've helped me learn to do HTML [hypertext markup language] and how to create an About Me page. . . . I consider them my extended family."

Café regulars often get together in person, exchange gifts, and have devised online Christmas parties involving several dozen people. More than a few have married. As one heavy-duty eBay user from western Michigan describes it:

> At the eBay Café you will meet a bunch of caring and friendly folks talking, helping, laughing, and at times even complaining about many varied subjects. I have found and met some great folks there. If you ever need help with almost ANYTHING, if you have some tips, tricks or a good story or two to share or you need help with a frustrating auction experience (yes they DO happen) join in, you may be yucking it up in just a few minutes. If you just need some people to talk to the Café is the place.

There are now plenty of auction sites on the Internet, and most have user bulletin boards and chat rooms. But none compare with the traffic of eBay's.

■ CUSTOMER SUPPORT

In the eBay business model, the real action takes place between members of the user community. The company participates only indirectly: as facilitator, rule-setter, and toll-taker. Other than automated billings and e-mails from eBay, relatively few interactions occur between the company and its millions of buyers and sellers. Nevertheless, a certain level of customer support is required, and the company has struggled to provide it as the number of users and auction transactions has exploded.

"How do I list an auction item?"

"Where do I upload the pictures?"

"Who pays shipping?"

"What can I do if the winner bidder fails to send payment?"

"Who should I call if I see a scam or prohibited auction?"

Users—particularly new ones—have lots of questions. And since a huge new echelon of novice users registers each quarter, the tasks of education, communicating tips, and simply helping people over the rough spots are endless.

Most customer service functions are so straightforward that they can be handled through self-service, using home-page hyperlinks. These are prominently located on the eBay home page, putting help for buyers and sellers only a click away (Figure 3.2).

But some aspects of customer support require a knowledgeable human respondent. Between 1995 and 1997, eBay hired independent contractors to handle these tasks. In this it was highly selective, hiring only people who were active, enthusiastic, and savvy users of the site—dyed-in-the-wool eBaysians. This concept fit right in with the com-

Figure 3.2 Home-page help. *(From eBay Web site. Used with permission.)*

munity theme; the company was paying users to help other users. These customer service representatives operated from their own homes, answered e-mail queries, and responded to questions placed by users on the eBay bulletin boards. Rotating schedules made it possible to provide service 7 days a week, 24 hours a day, every day.

Eventually, the company figured out that it would never really understand customer problems and control the quality of its customer service function if it did not employ and supervise its service representatives directly. Thus, beginning in 1997, it began training its own customer service reps, siting them in its San Jose headquarters. By early 1998, 40 service reps were on the payroll: 30 were remote independent contractors, and 10 were eBay employees. Within six months the numbers had grown to 70 remote reps and 30 employee reps in San Jose.[13] By mid-1999 the number of reps had expanded, and the company opened a customer service center in Salt Lake City, Utah, staffed with several hundred service reps and their supervisors. The remote, independent contractors remained, but policy dictated that all *new* hires would be sited in either the company's San Jose headquarters or its new service center.

➤ Voice of the Customer Day

eBay's executives know that their wealth and success depend entirely on the community of users and on their continued auction activity. To keep in touch with this community, its employees regularly scan bulletin boards that discuss new and altered site features, new categories, and so forth. Regular users, people who spend hours each day on eBay, are also brought to the San Jose headquarters at regular intervals, where employees get a chance to meet them and solicit their views.[14]

■ LESSONS FROM EBAY

eBay and its buyers and sellers have built a unique community from which all benefit. It is clear that the site would never have achieved its current success without that sense of community. As founder Omidyar once told a convention of collectors, "What eBay is today is what you've built. What eBay will be tomorrow is what you'll create."[15] As we will see in Chapter 8, major auction site rivals have failed to build similar communities of interest, which may account for their limited commercial success to date.

eBay's challenge moving forward is to maintain its sense of community among users as the number of participants expands in numbers and across national boundaries—as the small town grows into a metropolis. John Perry Barlow, cofounder of the Electronic Frontier Foundation, believes this is quite possible, citing his own neighborhood in New York City, a vibrant community within a huge metropolitan area. "Like New York, eBay has lots of neighborhoods. You've got the neighborhood of stamp collectors, the neighborhood of Pokemon collectors, glass elephant collectors, and so forth. If you look at those little enclaves, they seem very much like communities."[16]

So, what can your business learn from the eBay community and the mechanisms that bind it together? Would greater community between you and your customers (and with your supply chain partners) benefit all parties? If the answer is yes, how could you create such a community?

As noted earlier, customers of traditional businesses rarely feel any sense of community with those companies or with fellow customers. There are some exceptions. When the newly designed Volkwagen Beetle was introduced a few years back, owners of the squat little vehicle would honk at each other in recognition. But that spirit of vehicular fraternity faded once the novelty wore off. Macintosh owners, a persistent bunch to say the least, also have the trappings of a user community, complete with their own magazines, conferences in major cities, and online chat rooms where they can share tips, gossip, air complaints, and cast spells on Microsoft's evil empire and its lackeys. Many Mac users would prefer being boiled in oil to owning a Wintel machine.

Perhaps the best model of community building in the world of traditional business can be found at Harley-Davidson. Harley's instrument of community building is the Harley Owners Group, or HOG ("500,000 Members—1 Passion"). HOG members by the thousands participate in events sponsored by the company and HOG chapters scattered throughout the United States and Europe. These events give Harley motorcycle owners opportunities to interact, learn from each other, and drink from the same bottle of Ripple. They also provide a forum in which users can interact on a person-to-person basis with Harley engineers, market researchers, and the social anthropologists employed by the company to study and interpret the tribal ways of Harley folk.

Any company that's serious about its customers and their continued loyalty could learn a great deal from the Harley experience. Harley could also learn much from the eBay experience. For example, an online chat room sited on the Harley home page and a proprietary auction site for used parts, accessories, and HOG memorabilia seem eminently feasible.

Could you do something similar for your business? Think about it.

Chapter

4

The eBay Business Model

■ ALTERNATIVE MODELS ■ PARTNERS AND SUPPLIERS
■ HOW INVESTORS SEE IT ■ BUSINESS MODEL LESSONS

It's doubtful that Pierre Omidyar had the telephone industry in mind when he worked out the design of his new
company, but both follow a similar approach to generating revenues and profits. Neither sells nor produces
anything, but both have created *systems* through which
customers can interact. And both charge for the privilege
of using these systems. eBay's model for generating operating income is conceptually simple:

Net revenues (from seller fees)
− Cost of net revenues (infrastructure)
− Operating expenses (marketing, product
development, general and administrative,
and amortization)
= Operating income

Almost from Day 1, this business model has produced
positive and growing operating income and, after taxes,
bottom-line profits for eBay shareholders. Those bottom-

71

line profits grew to $10.8 million in 1999, not bad for a small team of some 300 employees, though abysmally thin for a company with eBay's stratospheric market valuation (Figure 4.1). Nevertheless, real and growing profits in an industry noted for megalosses has provided assurance to eBay shareholders. Internet rival Amazon, by comparison, could show its investors nothing but a string of cumulative losses through 1999 totaling nearly half a billion dollars—with no profits in sight.

Jamie Kiggen, director of Internet research for Donaldson, Lufkin & Jenrette, began following eBay in mid-1997 when it was still a small private company. "We were struck by what a large opportunity this company represented," he recalled in our interview. "I thought it was probably the most powerful business model I had seen. It combined the scalability of Amazon's model—the ability to grow revenues at a very rapid rate—with the profitability of Yahoo!'s model. That was a combination we hadn't come across in a young Internet company."

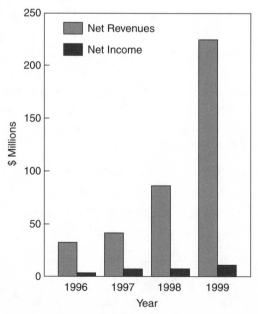

Figure 4.1 eBay revenues and profitability, 1996–1999.
(From eBay, Inc., 1999 Form 10-K filing.)

The financial model wasn't the only thing that impressed Kiggen. He was struck by the loyalty of the user base, by the number of people who had built their own businesses thanks to eBay, and by the "word-of-mouth buzz" they created for the company. "I hadn't come across anything like it before."

Until 2000, eBay's revenues came entirely from user fees paid by auction sellers. Unlike other online sites, there were no ads and, hence, no ad revenues. This is slowly changing. Bidders pay nothing. Sellers generally pay two types of fees: insertion fees and final value fees.

- *Insertion fee.* Sellers pay an insertion fee for every item listed for auction. The actual amount of the fee is based on either the seller's stipulated minimum bid or the reserve price. (Remember, the *reserve price* is a price below which the seller is not obliged to sell; it is hidden from bidders.) This insertion fee is non-refundable if an item fails to sell. However, a seller can apply for a credit if the item is relisted in another auction. Sellers who use reserve prices must also pay small added fees: $0.50 when the reserve price is less than $25, and $1 when it is greater than that amount. These fees are refunded when auctions are successfully consummated.

- *Final value fee.* When an auction is successfully completed, eBay's computers charge the seller another fee based on the amount of the winning bid. This fee begins at 5 percent of final value and declines in stepwise fashion for higher final values (see Table 4.1).

Real estate and vehicles auctioned on the site are subject to fixed insertion and final values fees. Real estate sellers, for example, must pay a $50 fee to be listed (with no final fee). Vehicle sellers pay a flat $25 to be listed and $25 if and when the vehicle is successfully auctioned. And if a seller wants an auction site to stand out of the crowd, he or she can pay a small fee to have it underlined or listed with an eye-catching icon such as "Hot" or "New."

TABLE 4.1 EBAY FEE RATES, 1999

Insertion Rates	
Minimum Bid or Reserve Price	**Fee**
$0.01–$9.99	$0.25
$10.00–$24.99	$0.50
$25.00–$49.99	$1.00
$50.00 and higher	$2.00

Final Value Rates	
Winning Bid	**Fee**
$25 or less	$5.00
$25.01–$1,000	First $25: 5%
	2% thereafter
Over $1,000	First $25: 5%
	$25.01–$1,000: 2.5%
	Over $1,000: 1.25%

These various fees fuel the eBay money machine, and have skyrocketed in aggregate as a function of the growing numbers of auctions posted on the site over the past few years. The toll collectors at eBay take a small piece of every transaction—not so much that it seriously discourages sellers from listing, but enough to generate huge revenues. During 1999, the company's average toll on site traffic was roughly 8 percent of the final value of auctioned merchandise.

With the number of competing sites fast increasing, and many charging *no* user fees as a strategy to grab market share, eBay is constrained from increasing its toll on site traffic. Thus, its only effective means of increasing revenues are (1) to increase traffic *volume* and (2) to expand into higher-priced categories of goods. The details of the company's strategies for pumping up volume and upscale expansion are described in Chapter 6.

Creating higher revenue, however, has not been eBay's main challenge. Net revenues have grown like wildfire. But each unit of revenue growth has been more and more

REVENUE SOURCES FOR ONLINE AUCTION SITES

In 1999, Forrester Research studied 30 online auction sites, both person-to-person and business-to-consumer, to determine their sources of revenue. As with eBay, other auction sites looked to seller fees for the lion's share of their revenues, but some sites garnered revenues from ads and product sales.

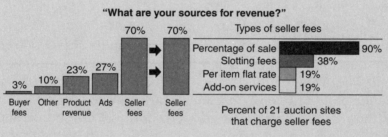

Auction revenue sources. *(From "Consumers Catch Auction Fever," Forrester Research, March 1999, p. 4. Used with permission.)*

costly and, as a percentage of net revenues, eBay's income from operations has progressively dwindled. As Table 4.2 indicates, both the cost of net revenues and operating expenses have increased at a much faster rate than net revenues, putting a big squeeze on operating income. That squeeze has caused operating margins to tumble from 24 percent in 1997 to 6 percent in 1998 and to −0.01 percent in 1999. Only interest income prevented the company from taking a loss in that final year.

The cause of the big squeeze is clear: aggressive investments in Web infrastructure, sales and marketing, product development, and acquisitions. General and administrative expenses also rose, but much less dramatically as a percentage of revenues. A good case can be made for these investments. Like an aggressive army, eBay's strategy is to move quickly to capture territory and key positions in the new

TABLE 4.2   THE BIG SQUEEZE

Parameter	1996	1997	1998	1999
Total revenues	$32,051	$41,370	$86,129	$224,724
Cost of net revenues	6,803	8,404	16,094	57,588
Operating expenses	18,826	22,983	57,270	168,300
Amortization				1,145
Merger-related costs				4,359
Operating income (loss)	$ 6,420	$ 9,983	$12,765	($ 1,164)

Note: All figures in thousands.
Source: eBay, Inc., 1999 Form 10-K filing.

world of online auctions before opposing forces can do so, the costs be damned. Once those key positions are taken and consolidated, according to this strategy, control and defense of conquered market terrain can be accomplished with far fewer expenditures and resources. Competitors will find eBay deeply entrenched and difficult to dislodge, and margins will return to enviable levels. The business model itself makes this strategy feasible. "We don't take title to the inventory," CEO Whitman told *Upside* in a 1999 interview, "so our costs of goods sold are largely customer support and site depreciation."

> We start with a very high gross margin, and my 20 years in business tells me that when you start with a high gross margin, everything else falls into place. When you start with a low gross margin, it's really hard to make money. [At] Hasbro, the difference between a 40 percent gross margin and a 42 percent gross margin on a toy made all the difference in the world, and you [would] fight to squeeze out that extra point. The fact that we started [eBay] with a very healthy gross margin gives us flexibility to spend money where we need to.[1]

As operating income progressively withered as a percentage of total revenues, investors and Wall Street analysts wondered if the eBay money machine had lost its punch. Many predicted that eBay would have to continue its aggressive spending on branding and infrastructure as competition grew more intense, causing a string of lackluster performances. These perceptions caused eBay stock to take a stomach-wrenching 64 percent drop in value at one point.

Despite declining margins, eBay executives remained confident in early 2000 that heavy investments in brand building, service, product development, and infrastructure would eventually pay off. And once the pace of those investments slowed down, the lion's share of cash flow from revenues would drop to the bottom line like a ton of bricks. At least one analyst supported their view when he wrote in late 1999 that "We believe the worst may be over for the Company's recent gross margin deterioration, which could show marked improvement this quarter [of 2000]."[2]

■ ALTERNATIVE MODELS

eBay's model simply provides a forum in which users—sellers and buyers—can conduct business. It does not act as a *principal* in these transactions—that is, it has no ownership interest in the goods sold at auction. Nor does it act as agent for eBay sellers. It is totally neutral. This neutral status eliminates many of the functions that concern other businesses. It holds no inventory. It has no responsibility for the goods offered at auction, for collecting buyers' payment, or for shipping. Its only responsibilities are to maintain the integrity of the auction process and the information linkages that make it feasible, and to bill and collect the fees it charges sellers.

A look around the Internet reveals a number of competing models. One of these is Egghead's Online.com, which has created one of the most popular consumer sites on the Internet, attracting almost 6 million site visits between November 15 and December 19 of 1999 alone, according to Nielsen/NetRatings. Ernst & Young estimates

FIRST TO SCALE AND THE NETWORK EFFECT

eBay was not the first in the online auction market, but it was first to scale—that is, first to operate efficiently and effectively on a massive volume of transactions. This fact has compounded the problems faced by dangerous competitors like Amazon and Yahoo!, neither of which has succeeded in building anything near eBay's user base.

Since the beginning, the prevailing wisdom has dictated that whichever site is first to capture a dominant share of buyers and sellers—and scale up an infrastructure capable of reliably handling their transactions—will own the future. According to this view, buyers will be attracted to the dominant site because it offers the most products to bid on, and sellers will be attracted to it because it is where they will find the most buyers. The site will enjoy a *network effect*: more buyers will attract more sellers, and vice versa.

So far, the prevailing wisdom has proven correct. The many auction site users interviewed in the course of writing this book indicated that the network effect is not simply a theoretical concept. "I list my auction on eBay," sellers volunteered, "because that's where the buyers are." And buyers said that they go "where the most items are listed."

that buyers spent an average of $217 on this site during that holiday period.

Online.com was the brainchild of Web entrepreneurs Jerry Kaplan and Alan Fisher. Back in 1994, when Online was founded, major retailers and mail order companies— L.L. Bean and Lands' End among them—were struggling to develop volume businesses on the Web. They were developing attractive Web sites and fulfillment mechanisms. The merchandise they offered and the prices they charged, however, were no different than those they offered customers through their regular distribution channels. It was the same stuff at the same prices. The only difference was that customers were ordering online rather than through a catalog and 800 number.

To Kaplan and Fisher, these retailers were failing to exploit the benefits of the new medium. Their innovation was to bring a different class of merchandise to the Web, and to let supply and demand determine prices.

Initially, Online sold a selection of excess, close-out, and refurbished consumer electronics products. This satisfied the need of manufacturers to unload wasting inventories and the desire of consumers to find bargains. But knowing what these items were worth was hard for *anyone* to know—buyers or sellers. What, for example, was a Pentium II PC worth when all the manufacturers were rolling out their Pentium III–based models. No one knew for sure. The only certainty was that the market value of these PCs melted away like ice on a hot day as they sat in the warehouse. An online auction was the perfect format for pricing these items and moving them out of inventory. It was quick, efficient, and required no costly advertising, creating a win-win for buyers and sellers.

By continually rotating the available merchandise, and creating a sense of scarcity and "get it while it lasts," Kaplan and Fisher made their auctions interesting and fun, and that remains true today. Their first auction took place in May 1995. By 1999, Online had expanded its offering to sporting goods and vacations, and made these available through two online "stores": Onsale atAuction and Onsale atCost. Onsale atAuction provided opportunities for users to bid on more than 1,400 different excess, close-out, and refurbished items each day. Onsale atCost, in contrast, featured a broad selection of *new* computers and computer-related products in a nonauction format. But instead of offering these at the traditional retailer's markup, atCost offered them at its wholesale invoiced price *plus* a transaction fee, a payment processing fee, shipping fees, and applicable taxes. The breakdown of these charges was made available to customers. Here, in contrast to an eBay auction, Onsale was acting as the seller. This was *not* a person-to-person transaction.

To complicate things further, Onsale's auction and direct-sales goods are today offered under two different arrangements: principal sales and agent sales. These arrangements are irrelevant to buyers but highly relevant to Onsale's model for generating revenues and profits.

- *Principal sales.* In a principal sale, Onsale owns the merchandise, which may be held in its own inventory or by the vendor. Onsale charges the successful bidder's credit card, then either ships the merchandise or directs the vendor to do so. As the legal owner, it assumes the price and obsolescence risk associated with the merchandise. When computer and other high-tech equipment is involved, these related risks can be high. By some estimates, the value of this class of equipment shrinks at an average of 2 percent every week that it sits on the shelf. Some principal sales are actually consignment sales in which Onsale takes ownership once a purchase has been made. The consignment sale eliminates the risks associated with holding inventory.

- *Agent sale.* In an agent sale transaction, the merchandise is owned by a third-party vendor, who is responsible for collecting the winning payment and shipping the merchandise. Onsale has nothing at risk in these agent transactions, and collects a commission for sale of the merchandise.

Onsale also generates a small revenue stream from advertising, market development funds, and discounts from vendors.

Onsale's business model depends heavily on an ability to offer a continuous and varied stream of attractive merchandise. If site visitors are not interested in the merchandise, or if they see the same old things every time they enter the site, they will drift away. Realizing this, Onsale employs a staff of experienced buyers who keep in close contact with vendors. Their job is to bring the best and the freshest vendor merchandise to the site.

Onsale's relationship with its suppliers—its "sellers"—is probably the most critical difference between its business model and that of eBay. It actively engages manufacturers and service providers with the goal of creating *supply* on its site. Get the supply online, it figures, and the buyers will follow. The supply stream of excess merchandise, however, ebbs and flows and cannot be controlled. The release of new generation of chips by Intel creates PC close-outs aplenty. But that initial flow of goods is often followed by a trickle.

eBay, in contrast, appears to have taken the advice offered to actor Kevin Costner in the movie *Field of Dreams*. That character had doubts about his obsession to build a baseball field in the cornfield surrounding his home. "Build it," he was told, "and they will come." eBay's model appears to take the same approach to buyers and sellers. Build the auction site, and they will come. And they have, in growing numbers. Can eBay proactively bring more sellers and buyers to its site? Yes, but only through indirect means—by creating greater public awareness of the site (more on this in Chapter 6).

■ PARTNERS AND SUPPLIERS

Most business designs today—both in conventional manufacturing and in the new world of e-commerce—create value for customers through carefully structured and managed supplier-partner relationships. These relationships have always existed, but rarely commanded the importance they do today.

The rationale for partnerships is straightforward. Today's customers want some combination of *faster, cheaper,* and *better,* but few companies have either the know-how or the resources to deliver on all three. If they break apart the value chain, however, and assign each link to whomever can do it best, fastest, and at the least cost, they have a good chance of truly satisfying customers and crushing their competitors. This approach is very different than the vertical integration of value chain activities that characterized the Industrial Age, when companies like U.S. Steel and Ford Motor Company owned and controlled almost every step of the manufacturing process. Henry Ford, for example, was so controlling that he owned the farms that supplied food for his assembly plants' cafeterias. Vertical integration in a world driven by technological change and buyer power rarely makes sense.

David Bovet and Joe Martha of Mercer Management Consulting have coined the term *value net* to describe the most advanced supplier-partner relationships. In their definition, "a *value net* is a business design that relies on advanced supply chain concepts to deliver superior customer satisfaction and company profitability. It is a fast, flexible system that is aligned and driven by customer choice."[3] As they point out, value nets bring together one company with a compelling value proposition and one or more others that contribute to rapid response, profit capture, and flawless execution. These nets are collaborative, scalable to the level of the expanding business, fast, and linked to customers through information technology.

Gateway is a prime example of value net business design, and Bovet and Martha describe it in compelling terms. Like rival Dell, its customers communicate their preferences directly, mostly through an online *choice board* on which they configure the PCs they want. Once made and confirmed by purchasers, those choices are communicated electronically to Gateway and its tight circle of component suppliers. Because every specification is included in the customer's order, Gateway and its hub suppliers can move the custom-built PC through the assembly operation and to the customer's doorstep in about five business days. This is possible, in large part, because of Gateway's network of effective value chain partners—from its component and software suppliers to the United Parcel Service (UPS) personnel who handle all customer-bound logistics. This network operates with about as much clockwork precision as one can expect in a global manufacturing enterprise, and explains why Gateway is profitable and growing in an industry choking with capacity, competition, and thin margins.

While Gateway makes the most of a supplier network, it maintains exclusive control of its interface with customers through its home-page choice board, phone order facility, customer service, and a worldwide network of Gateway Country stores. That interface is the most valuable part of the entire value network because it is Gateway's exclusive link with real demand and changing customer requirements. eBay likewise rigorously controls its interface with customers, using its home page as the mechanism. This control assures that customers get the right messages about the company and its services, and that the company has exclusive contact with and knowledge of its customer base. At the same time, it outsources value-creating activities that customers never see to suppliers.

eBay's most important outsourced activity is Web hosting. Web hosting creates the electronic interface between a site and the Internet. And for any company that gets a million hits each day, it is a critical activity requiring major capital investment and technical personnel. eBay's Web-hosting function is outsourced to AboveNet and Exodus Communications, two major service providers and leaders in hosting large-volume Web sites. These suppliers maintain front-end Web servers, which feed into eBay's proprietary database and applications servers, which are located at the suppliers' facilities. According to Prabakar Sundarrajan, Exodus's vice president of research and development, eBay's technical personnel visit his company's Santa Clara facilities periodically to upgrade or troubleshoot, but rely on Exodus technicians to manage day-to-day operations. Contrary to what one would expect in this type of arrangement, eBay owns its own servers; it merely operates them from its suppliers' facilities.

Essentially invisible to the general public, Web hosters like Exodus and AboveNet form key links in the backbone of the Internet economy. Operating out of custom-designed, temperature-controlled facilities with seismically braced server racks, state-of-the-art fire suppression and security systems, and redundant power sources, they aim to keep client sites up and running 24 hours a day, 7 days a week. And they serve many clients, including direct competitors. Exodus, for example, serves eBay, but is also a primary service provider for rival Yahoo! as well as Lycos, CBS SportsLine, Nordstrom, and other major online companies.

Outsourcing has several benefits for eBay:

- Outsourcing Internet infrastructure tasks allows it to better focus on its core business.
- It experiences cost savings through economies of scale and cost sharing, and can purchase servers and other equipment at lower prices through its hosting suppliers.
- The problem of recruiting and retaining scarce technical personnel can be minimized. Because the demand for competent technical people far outstrips supply, it generally makes sense to engage them through specialized vendors. "It's very difficult for companies to find expertise," Exodus's Sundarrajan told me. "It's very difficult to find the network designers, the security people, the facilities operators, and people like that, and to scale up as they need to."
- Vendors like Exodus and AboveNet have the wherewithal to help their clients scale up rapidly.

While eBay's infrastructure suppliers provide fee-based services directly to the company, other third-party providers deal directly with site users. These providers include the following:

- *e-Stamp.* Postage is a big issue for volume sellers in the United States, particularly since U.S. Postal Service rules require that all stamped packages weighing more than 16 ounces must be handed directly to a postal clerk. They cannot be dropped into a postal box. This policy goes back to the years in which the Unabomber killed or maimed a number of people by means of package bombs delivered through the Postal Service. Though the Unabomber was caught and imprisoned, the policy remains. And thousands of eBay sellers must stand in long lines each day in order to comply with it.

  Recognizing that time is a key asset for its sellers, eBay developed a relationship with e-Stamp, a Postal Service–approved service that allows people to buy and print postage online. e-Stamp allows people to ship packages via first-class, parcel post, priority, and express mail. More important, parcels with e-stamps are exempt from the Postal Service's security regulation. Postal carriers can pick them up, and packages weighing up to five pounds can be dropped into Postal Service mail boxes. For many eBay sellers, this eliminates the daily trip to the post office. Packages too large for mail boxes or for postal carriers can be dropped off in post office bins without having to wait in line.

- *iShip.* Auction winners generally pay shipping charges, and they generally like to know how much these charges will be. No one likes big surprises. So eBay has arranged with iShip, a third-party provider to help buyers estimate shipping rates.

- *Mailbox Etc.* This nationwide chain of package shippers provides custom packaging and shipping arrangement for eBay users, who receive special discounts of 10 to 15 percent.

- *iEscrow.* As described in the previous chapter, iEscrow is a third-party escrow holder which eBay buyers and sellers can use at their option to assure the security of their transactions, funds, and goods.

- *Billpoint.*   In March 2000, eBay teamed up with Wells Fargo Bank to provide one of the services most needed by both buyers and sellers: secured online credit-card transactions. Instead of paying with bank checks, or delaying shipment until their personal checks clear, buyers can now pay with their credit cards and have their items shipped immediately.

The eBay business model is linked to still other strategic partners: AOL, Disney, AutoTrade.com, CarClub, and others. We'll discuss these relationships in Chapter 6.

Figure 4.2 shows a graphic representation of eBay's connected network of customers, company, and partners. Here, buyers, sellers, and eBay are in touch through an online interface maintained by the company and its auction-hosting suppliers. Links allow buyers and sellers to deal with other providers, and they communicate with each other through Internet e-mail.

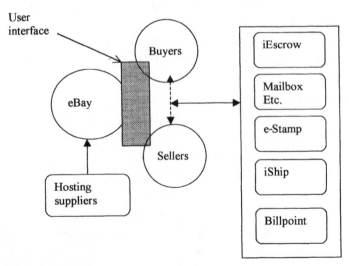

Figure 4.2   eBay's value network.

eBay's outsourcing and partnering reflects strategic choices to:

- Focus personnel on customer-oriented issues and market opportunities
- Minimize investments in fixed assets
- Remain small and agile as an organization

The net result of these choices is a very lean operation that can handle close to $3 billion in merchandise transactions with a payroll of only a few hundred employees. Unburdened by layers of personnel and management, it can make decisions quickly—an absolute must in a fast-changing environment. Moreover, its financial resources can be directed toward business-building activities instead of being tied up in either inventory or substantial fixed assets. A comparison with Amazon, which has a very different business model, underscores this point (Table 4.3). eBay is free of inventory, and only a small portion of its total assets are bound up in fixed assets. Most of its assets take the form of cash, securities, and receivables, which are available for strategic acquisitions, customer service initiatives, product development, brand building, and other

TABLE 4.3 INVENTORY AND FIXED ASSETS AS A PERCENTAGE OF TOTAL CORPORATE ASSETS: EBAY VERSUS AMAZON, AS OF DECEMBER 31, 1999

Parameter	eBay	Amazon
Inventory*	$ 0	$ 220.7
Fixed assets*	$ 111.8	$ 317.6
Total assets*	$963.9	$2,471.5
Total assets dedicated to inventory and fixed assets	11.6%	21.8%

*Figures in thousands.
Source: Amazon.com, Inc., and eBay, Inc., 1999 Form 10-K filings.

business-building activities. In Amazon's model, a much higher percentage of total assets is locked up in inventory, property, and equipment. This may be just the right thing to do for Amazon, given its goals and operating model, but asset intensity has made it less agile in changing course, less able to scale up or down in response to real customer demand, and more risky to its shareholders. And risk increases the cost of capital—even the cost of equity—because shareholders demand a higher return from riskier investments.

■ HOW INVESTORS SEE IT

By all accounts, investors and analysts are comfortable with eBay's business model. It is simple yet sufficiently robust to respond to rapid growth and a changing competitive terrain. What keeps their stomachs churning are concerns over the particular metrics that determine share value in the frothy world of dot-com investing, a world in which traditional benchmarks of value have been tossed overboard.

In the past, investors generally valued companies as some multiple of current net earnings (profits). For example, among the Standard & Poor's 500-Stock Index (S&P 500) companies the ratio between the average share price and earnings per share has generally hovered around 15 to 1—that is, share values have been around $15 for every $1 of current earnings. This ratio fluctuates with the mood of investors—with respect to both particular companies and the stock market in general. Optimism drives the ratio higher, and pessimism causes it to sag.

For young companies that produce few or no earnings, the price-to-earnings benchmark is rightfully abandoned as inappropriate as long as investors see realistic prospects for high and growing *future* earnings. Ryan Jacob, manager of the Jacob Internet Fund, summed it up when he told the

Industry Standard that profits are "not terribly important. What matters is projections of future earnings."

After all, it is the future that matters because the future is what the *next* owner of the shares will be buying. In these cases, the price-to-sales ratio is often a better measure of value, a notion argued forcefully in the 1980s by money manager Ken Fisher.[4] By the price-to-sales ratio, eBay was capitalized in early 2000 by a whooping $121 for every dollar of current sales. Its peer group of Internet big-timers—Amazon and Yahoo!—enjoyed equally stratospheric valuations.

The only justification for very high price-to-sales ratios is the belief (the hope) that Internet companies will eventually grow into the outsized valuations they currently enjoy (see Figure 4.3). This is a bit like spending $1,000 on a size-40 Brooks Brothers suit for your 8-year-old

---

WHACKO VALUATION YARDSTICKS?

Cast adrift from the time-honored measures of stock value, the prognosticators of the Internet market have invented new ones such as "market value per customer" and "market value per page view"—neither of which has been tested through an entire market cycle.

Alfred Rappaport, emeritus professor of Northwestern University's Kellogg School of Management and unofficial dean of shareholder value specialists, eschews both traditional and newly hatched value measures in favor of *free cash flow,* which he defined as cash earnings minus cash outflows for fixed- and working-capital investments—where cash earnings are earnings before deducting noncash items, such as depreciation and amortization. He urges investors to focus on free cash flow, noting that while traditional companies typically experience earnings and investment outflows, "some young Internet companies generate just the reverse—losses and investment inflows."[5]

EBAY	Ebay Inc					6/2/2000
Last:	Change:	Open:	High:	Low:	Volume:	
77 3/16	9 13/16	71 7/8	77 1/4	70 5/8	4,992,000	
	Percent Change:	Yield:	P/E Ratio:	52 Week Range:		
	14.56%	n/a	1,543.75	35.1406 to 124.875		

Figure 4.3 eBay price and volume fluctuations. Chart reflects a 2-for-1 stock split effective May 24, 2000. *(From www.bigcharts.com. Reproduced with permission.)*

son, figuring that it may fit him when he grows up. Of course, paying today for tomorrow's anticipated profitability doesn't leave a lot of room for upside appreciation, and it exposes the investor to the very real possibility that these companies may never fulfill their growth expectations. Referring to dot-com businesses from the vantage point of April 2000, Harvard Business School professor Michael Porter said that "We are in a phase where the fundamental rules of economics and competition are being temporarily suspended, but they aren't going to be suspended for much longer."[6]

In early 2000, lots of people wondered if the high-flying Internet stocks would *ever* grow into their suits. "No sector of the stock market has generated more euphoria and more skepticism," Alfred Rappaport told *Wall Street Journal* readers.[7] Fed Chairman Allan Greenspan's view was unambiguous: "Investing in Internet stocks is like playing the lotteries." Many saw the market for Internet stocks as a classic speculative bubble, and complained that investors and securities analysts alike were too intoxicated with success to see the coming collapse.

The NASDAQ collapse of mid-April 2000 underscored the validity of their concerns, wiping out more than 20 percent of the composite index's value. Many dot-coms saw their market capitalizations cut in half in just a few days.

Several months earlier, Steven Rosner, a vice president of LEK Consulting, calculated the future cash-flow growth in the period 2003 to 2013 required to justify the prevailing valuations of Amazon, Yahoo, and eBay.[8] According to Rosner, Amazon needed to grow revenues at an annual rate of 38 percent between 2003 and 2013. He noted that even fast-growing companies like Intel, Microsoft, Wal-Mart, and Home Depot had been *unable* to sustain that rate of growth. If Amazon somehow managed to pull off this miracle, it would reach $100 billion in revenues in 2013. "That would exceed the entire forecasted U.S. market for books and music in 2013 ($85 billion) and account for between 30 percent and 50 percent of worldwide sales in these categories." Yahoo, though profitable, would have to sustain a neck-breaking 56 percent growth in revenues to grow into its current valuation, per Rosner.

Nor was Mr. Rosner's analysis of eBay valuation any more optimistic. "Assuming commissions stay at 6 percent," he wrote, "eBay's annual revenue growth rate will need to be 62 percent between 2003 and 2013 in order to justify a market cap of $19 billion. At that rate, eBay's 2013 revenues would be $55 billion, based on $920 billion worth of goods sold [at auction]—and would account for more than three percent of the entire expected U.S. nominal Gross Domestic Product."

Even if this analysis is only halfway correct, investors have to ask: Will eBay eventually grow into the high market valuation it enjoys in early 2000? Only time will tell, but its success depends on two things: continued revenue growth and breaking through the big squeeze on operating profits. As we will see in Chapter 6, the company's strategy to expand its user base and to move into higher-priced goods categories represent its best hope for success.

■ BUSINESS MODEL LESSONS

eBay's business model has proven its worth as a mechanism for generating revenues and converting them into profits. This is essentially a toll-taking model. It has created an infrastructure and charges users a toll. As such, it is suitable for only a very small number of commercial enterprises. Nevertheless, you may find lessons applicable to your company in this model. Here are a few possibilities:

- If portions of your value chain—be they fulfillment, manufacturing, or assembly—can be done faster, quicker, or better by others, engage those others as value net partners. Structure a win-win relationship between your company, these partners, and your customers. Outsourcing noncore functions also frees up time, capital, and managerial attention for those aspects of your business that will get you ahead and keep you there: product development, customer acquisition, and so forth.

  However, think twice about surrendering any control of your customer interface. The customer interface is your pipeline into the characteristics and needs of your customers. It is a two-way medium through which you and they can communicate and develop lasting relationships. Don't let go of it.

- Depending on the nature of your business, it may be smart to minimize your fixed assets when and where you can. Fixed assets give you operating leverage in times of rising demand, but they are a dead weight when demand slackens. They also inhibit your ability to change rapidly in response to changes in technology and markets. If possible, pay someone else to handle your infrastructure.

- Create switching barriers for existing customers. Few innovative companies have anything that cannot be replicated by fast-following competitors. One way to keep your customers from going over to those competitors is to build switching barriers into your business model. eBay has done this with its feedback rating system—though perhaps without intending it. Once a user (particularly a volume seller) establishes a high feedback rating on eBay, he or she is reluctant to walk away and start from scratch on Yahoo!Auctions or some other site. This is not a hypothesis, but has been confirmed through seller comments on the site's discussion boards.

  Chances are that your business has opportunities to create switching barriers for current customers. Some companies use affinity and frequent purchase programs or free software that locks people in. What besides offering a great product and good service can you do to keep customers with you?

- Finally, make your business model scalable to demand—structure your business so that it can expand or contract as *actual* customer demand rises and falls. In the old days, companies buffered changes in demand with excess capacity and inventory. These, unfortunately, tied up assets and dissipated profits. Today's leading companies deal with demand changes through value net supplier relationships and mass customization.

Chapter

Inside eBay

The Internet economy has already created hundreds of thousands of new jobs in the United States, and the same is happening elsewhere in the world. This is undoubtedly just the beginning. Some of the people filling these new jobs are newly minted programmers, engineers, and managers. Many others, however, are migrants from the so-called old economy. Like the forty-niners of nineteenth-century America, these people have sensed high opportunity in the gold fields of Silicon Valley and other dot-com hotbeds, and are setting out to stake their claims. Salaries are low, but the chances of striking it rich on options are tangible—assuming that stock prices hold up through post-IPO lockup periods.

The first wave of fortune hunters, as in the earlier gold rush, was dominated by the young, the restless, and the unburdened (no mortgages, no families)—Generation Xers, in a modern Children's Crusade. This is changing as more and more mid- and upper-level managers and technical professionals are sprucing up their resumes and following the wagon trails carved out by the first wave. The skills they bring from the old economy are more and more in demand as Internet companies grow, mature, and discover that they need experience and technical know-how in marketing, corporate finance, and human resource management. Staffing at eBay reflects this trend. With the exception of founders Pierre Omidyar and Jeff Skoll, most of eBay's key executives came over from the managerial ranks of traditional business: Meg Whitman from Hasbro; Matt Bannick, vice president of customer service, from McKinsey & Company; CFO Gary Bengier from Kenetech Corporation, an energy service firm; and Marketing Senior Vice President Brian Swette from Pepsi-Cola.

Making the transition from the old economy to the new is not always easy, and some migrants find the move rockier than do others. According to Tuck Rickards, leader of Internet practice for Russell Reynolds Associates, an executive recruitment firm, "The person looking for a VP of marketing or chief of technology position needs to be Web savvy [whereas] the distribution specialist or operations person will probably find his previous experiences more transferable."

Migrants from the old economy encounter a very different working environment. Energy levels are high, and employees, like grad students on a burn, put in grueling hours. Real life and work life merge. The stakes are huge, and everyone aims to be a big winner. The organization structures they encounter are also tangibly different. Dot-com companies almost universally have loose structures and very little hierarchy or formality. Even the great and near-great work out of cubicles, including Yahoo! co-founder David Filo, whose working arrangement Po Bronson describes vividly in *The Nudist on the Night Shift* (Random House, 1999), his excellent portrait of Silicon Valley:

> David Filo doesn't even have an office. He shares a double-wide cubicle with another guy. It's a win-

dow cubicle, but located right on the thick support pillar, so there are only a couple feet of tinted window on either side. David was standing up, and he was awash in a trash heap of paper . . . forty inches deep of unread memos, promotional literature, office chatter.[1]

Because eBay would not make its executives available for interviews, or let me roam the corridors, and no ex-employees could be located, this "inside look" at the company is, by necessity, based on secondary interview sources and observations of company activities. While less than perfect, these nevertheless provide useful insights into what actually goes on. What we see through our win-

---

A WARNING

"Every company in America is going to be on the Internet [and] in involved in e-commerce," said Harvard Business School professor Michael Porter in April 2000. "The dot-com companies were the first, because the new enterprise can always move faster. But the more traditional companies are coming on strong. . . . Everybody's going to be doing it."

Nevertheless, new migrants to the gold fields of the Internet may find the best claims already staked out. Porter considered the great market euphoria of 1998 to 2000, in which many young employees profited immensely from stock options—at least on paper—as being "very fragile" and probably short-lived. "The early people who are there at round one can do enormously well, but that doesn't mean that this will be a good or profitable arena for young people going into it now. . . . Whenever Harvard Business School students are thronging into a particular field it's already past the peak. We had that in real estate. We had that in consulting and investment banking."[2]

dow, however, conforms closely with the general picture of Internet companies described here.

■ COHERENCE OF PRINCIPLES

When Pierre Omidyar conceived of his auction community as one reflecting values of honesty, openness, equality, empowerment, trust, mutual respect, and mutual responsibility, he expected that his new company would embrace the same values. As he told interviewers from Harvard Business School, "Internally, we *have* to share the same values as our community because we indirectly influence the community in everything we do."[3] In his view, every feature of the Web site, every press release, and every strategic partnership with other companies had to be consistent with the values of the community. And he looked to his employees to maintain those values among themselves and the senior management team. "We . . . encourage our employees to [speak out] if we're doing something that is not quite right. We've empowered everyone to be a guardian of the culture—everyone. It can't just be me. . . ."[4]

Inculcating this unique culture within the employee ranks is seen as a managerial responsibility. And it starts at the top, with Meg Whitman, who developed the practice of meeting every Monday morning with newly hired employees to explain eBay's values and how they, as employees, are expected to support it.

Openness, in Omidyar's view, means more than access. It implies a *no-penalty* operating culture in which fear of making a mistake, or fear of being on the wrong side of an issue, will not muzzle employees or subvert ideas that challenge the status quo. The importance of "driving out fear" from an organization is not new. W. Edwards Deming, one of the leaders of the quality movement, made it one of his famous 14 management principles in the 1970s.

Many companies pay lip service to this principle, but you have to wonder about how many honor it in practice.

■ DECISION MAKING

It's a safe bet that a company that encourages openness, insists on mutual respect, and tolerates mistakes will have a uniquely different way of making decisions. We'd assume that it would not tolerate screamers, table-pounders, people whose egos compel them to defend set positions, or executives who use their power to roll over opposing ideas. Instead, we'd expect to see a workplace in which decisions are made through a rational process that brings as many insights to the table as possible. David and Jim Matheson, consultants from nearby Menlo Park, California, suggested this type of culture in describing the *Smart Organization*.[5] The smart organization, in their definition, has rational and effective decision-making processes supported by nine cultural principles:

- Continual learning
- A focus on value creation
- An ability to develop creative alternatives
- Alignment and employee empowerment
- A disciplined process for weighing alternatives and making decisions
- Open information flow
- An outside-in strategic perspective
- A willingness to acknowledge and deal with uncertainty
- Systems thinking

Organizations that embrace these principles, according to the Mathesons' field research, are more successful at understanding their environments, mobilizing resources, and achieving their intended purposes.

Is eBay *smart?* Without having worked inside the company, it is impossible to know how many of these principles are operable—and it's doubtful that any company would embrace them all. But it is possible to see a few of them at work—in particular, empowerment and open information. "I've worked in a few companies where senior managers are so afraid of appearing weak that they stand by a point of view even in the face of better, more informed data," Meg Whitman recalled to interviewers. "At eBay, we have a no-penalty culture, meaning that there is no penalty for being on the wrong side of an issue or changing your mind in the face of better information. If you come to a meeting with one point of view and a colleague says something that convinces you that you're wrong, the culture is to say, 'O.K., that's smart. You're right. Let's move on.' "[6]

■ FOCUS AND SPEED

Being in new and unexplored terrain, Internet companies run into unanticipated problems and opportunities with startling regularity. Meg Whitman recognized this when she took the reins in early 1999. She knew that her management team would have to address and dispose of these quickly; doing otherwise would create a huge logjam of unresolved issues. With this in mind she instituted weekly management team meetings, each lasting up to four hours. "I figured out early on that if we were going to work together as a team we needed to throw the ball around a lot," she told Harvard case writers. "So we spend a lot of time together."[7] Time together included regularly scheduled companywide meetings. In the CEO's opinion, these meetings increased the level of familiarity and trust among managers to the point that decision making became faster and more effective. "We're now able to have pretty short and focused discussions, figure out what the points of view are, and make a decision quickly."[8]

As outsiders, we cannot observe eBay's decision-making processes or capabilities directly, but we can see their results, and these confirm Whitman's statement with respect to two dimensions of organizational decision making: strategic focus and speed.

➤ Focus

Like Amazon, Yahoo!, Priceline, and other Internet leaders, eBay has more investment opportunities than it can handle. This abundance would be a curse were it not for the company's clear understanding of its mission and its very tight focus on a handful of strategies. That mission—to be the world's largest person-to-person online auction company—is articulated repeatedly by senior management. All important decisions must be closely aligned with that mission. Likewise, the company has long embraced a handful of strategies for different aspects of its business: expanding the user base, strengthening the brand, broadening the trading platform, fostering community affinity, and enhancing site features and functionality (more on these in Chapter 6). Again, any tactical or policy decisions must advance one or more of these overarching strategies.

Clarity of mission and strategic focus make decision making faster and more effective. Decision making for some Internet rivals, particularly Amazon, which is attempting to be all things to all people, must be more difficult and time-consuming because of its broader mission.

➤ Speed

The importance of *time* cannot be overstated in the fast-changing world of e-commerce. If judged solely on the basis of its major public announcements, eBay is capable of making key decisions quickly. Indeed, one of the great challenges of analyzing eBay and preparing this book has been the company's continual stream of announcements on new programs, new site features, new policies, new acquisitions, new partnerships, and other major initiatives. These rapid-fire announcements reveal an organization that engages opportunities and problems quickly and disposes of them without a lot of hand-wringing or delay. Size and organizational simplicity certainly contribute to this. The quality of these decisions, however, remains to be seen.

■ MANAGING HYPERGROWTH

When *Upside*'s Chuck Lenatti asked Meg Whitman what kept her awake at night, she pointed to the problem of managing growth, and anticipating the changes that growth in Internet service would surely bring:

> One [concern] is managing the growth—predicting where we need to be 12 to 18 months from now and starting that process today. Hiring great people. Every incremental hire at eBay makes a difference today. Thinking about how the Internet is going to evolve, how the competitive landscape is going to change, what are the implications of broadband, what are the implications for eBay's product offering.[9]

No one at eBay, including Whitman or members of her team, has experienced anything approximating the pace of growth they are now charged with managing and sustaining. "Coming from land-based businesses—Hasbro, FTD, Stride Rite, Disney—to an Internet startup," she told *Fast Company*,

> I've had to get used to one major factor: the sheer rate of growth. We're growing at 40 percent to 50

percent *per quarter* [emphasis added]. That pace absolutely changes the leadership challenge: Every three months we become a different company. In one year, we went from 30 employees to 140, and from 100,000 registered users to 2.2. million. At Hasbro, we would set a yearlong strategy, and then we would simply execute against it. At eBay, we constantly revisit the strategy—and revise the tactics.[10]

The larger world of e-commerce is also growing and changing rapidly. How will the Internet evolve in the months and years ahead? How is the competitive landscape changing? This section looks at the issue of hypergrowth and how eBay and its people are responding to it.

Growth has been the preoccupation of U.S. executives ever since the mid-1990s, when they finally discovered that they couldn't downsize their companies to greatness. Traditionally, 15 percent in sales or earnings growth is accounted to be a major feat, even in buoyant economic times. Putting together a long *string* of 15-percent-growth years is even tougher. Among Fortune 1000 companies, that kind of growth generates generous bonuses and usually lands the CEO on the cover of *Fortune* or *BusinessWeek*. That level of growth, however, is paled by the eBay experience.

Rapid growth has been a mixed blessing for the company and its managers, for two reasons. First, eBay's stratospheric stock price has always been supported by expectations of *continued* super growth, and satisfying that expectation has driven eBay's strategy from its earliest days as a public company. Ever since the IPO, everyone has understood that any slackening of growth would damage confidence in the company, and its market value would take a nosedive. Thus, the company has never had the luxury of pausing in its meteoric rise to consolidate its gains or adjust to its greater size. A go-slow strategy has always been out of the question. Second, hypergrowth has created enormous stress on the company's management team. It must retain its current customers even as it adds new legions to their ranks every quarter. As Whitman told interviewers, "It's all about the battle for new consumers. That's why we have to grow faster than our competitors."[11] These new customers must be inculcated with the community spirit on which the company's success depends. But can this be possible when the company—its employee base, its auction infrastructure, and its customer service capabilities—is consumed with scaling up to meet skyrocketing demand?

➤ Maintaining Community Values

"Scaling the community and organization rapidly represents a major challenge in terms of being sure our values and culture are being communicated correctly," Whitman told interviewers in 1999.

> On the organizational side, we have to be sure we are hiring quality employees who fit with the culture—we can't afford to let that slip. On the external side, at the rate we are growing, we have more *new* people using the service in a quarter than the *total* number of people who had been using the service in the previous quarter. . . . How do the values of the community get communicated to those new people?[12]

Communicating company values for an organization of less than 400 people is not a major problem; it is clearly something over which management has considerable control, through its hiring decisions, and through the messages it sends to its work force every day. Transmitting those same values to the fast-growing user community is another question.

eBay's mechanisms for communicating its values to millions of active users are limited to e-mails and the various bulletin boards, newsletters, and announcements it places on its site. Site policies and its policing of certain behaviors are still other mechanisms. Each of these mechanisms is by nature indirect and weak. In the end, users must acculturate each other. This is a consequence of Omidyar's initial inspiration to base the community on openness, equality, empowerment, trust, and mutual responsibility.

In the early days, when the user community was small, eBay values were passed on to new users by veteran buyers and sellers, who took a proprietary attitude toward the site and its online protocol. Who will fill that role as the percentage of seasoned users is diluted by a rapid influx of new people? Won't the new people be interacting mostly with other novices? A visit to the chat rooms and discussion boards indicates that there are still plenty of dedicated auction veterans out in cyberspace providing guidance to newcomers and upholding the "this is our site" mentality. These mentors are serious hobbyists and small-business owners whose livings are tightly bound up with the site. They have every reason to see it continue and succeed.

➤ Scaling Up the Web Site

Imagine that you're a retailer and that 41,000 people entered your store during your first year of operation. The next year, 341,000 passed through the front door. This is great for business, but traffic inside the store and out in the parking lot is getting to be a problem. You hire an architect and a general contractor to begin work on store and parking-lot expansion. By the end of the third year, your customer count has exploded to 2.2 million, and people are piling up like sardines. A long queue of surly customers extends from the front door around the block. The customer count hits 10 million after the fourth year, and by now the line of people trying to get through your front door extends as far as the eye can see!

eBay isn't a retail store, but the preceding numbers describe the growth of its customer base (registered users) from 1996 through 1999. The number of auction listings and transactions during that period have followed a comparable rate of increase, creating a major infrastructure challenge for company management.

Increasing traffic volume on the eBay Web site requires constant expansion and upgrading of technology, transaction-processing systems, network infrastructure, and the engineering staff required to maintain it. Substantial capital outlays must be made to purchase and install servers with the company's Web-hosting suppliers. Any slackening in this effort could result in slow response times for users or possible service outages. The eBay community will tolerate neither.

Meg Whitman's first taste of the scaling-up problem occurred within a month of joining the firm, when the site went down and stayed down for eight hours. We can only imagine the sense of panic and frustration around the eBay shop on that day. The system had excess capacity and backup capabilities, but not enough to eliminate the potential for outages. Even then the system was servicing enormous daily demand: tens of millions of page view requests, 2 to 4 million searches, hundreds of thousands of individual bids, and e-mail communications. Moreover, an online auction has unique and difficult requirements that other systems do not face: constant processing and reprocessing of incoming bids. These place greater stresses on the site and reduce its stability.

One solution to the stability problem was to build substantial excess capacity, something that the company previously avoided. Overcapacity is costly, but Whitman viewed this cost as small relative to the cost of outages and poor Web-site performance. She translated that insight into a corporate goal of gradually building the system's infrastructure to 10 times needed capacity.

Scaling up a site infrastructure is a tricky business. When interviewed on this subject, officials of Exodus Communications, a key eBay Web-hosting supplier, would not disclose the actual capacity of eBay, its client. However, Research and Development Vice President Prabakar Sundarrajan said that "The key problem of growing in scale with demand [for Internet companies in general] is predicting what the demand will be. . . . You can't say that 'demand will grow by a certain factor.' It's not a smooth curve. You're going to have spikes and you're going to have unpredictable events [such as denial of service attacks]." He made the point that an Internet company also needs the *right kind* of capacity for the right kind of needs. Predicting those needs is problematic. "It's difficult to build overcapacity for everything."

Whitman's strategy of building excess capacity, however, seems to be paying off. During the highly visible denial-of-service attack against it and other major e-commerce sites in February 2000, eBay's problems were very limited. And by the spring of 2000, it appeared that the frequency and severity of past service outages was unlikely to repeat itself.

➤ Getting Big While Trying to Stay Small

eBay also faces the problem of hiring and training more and more people and inculcating them with its unique values. Armies and navies have demonstrated a capacity for doing this. During wartime in particular, they induct and indoctrinate huge influxes of new and untrained personnel. For example, during the first two years of World War II, the U.S. armed forces expanded from a small cadre of professional soldiers to a highly organized and effective force of several million. On the eve of that war, the U.S. Marine Corps was smaller than the New York City police force. By 1943 it had hundreds of thousands of trained personnel under arms and deployed in the South Pacific. Even more remarkable, each of the major U.S. military services, particularly the navy and marines, succeeded in passing on its unique practices and traditions to a deluge of newcomers for whom military manners, attitudes, and procedures were entirely alien. Their keys to scaling up were (and continue to be) training systems, codified operating procedures, and a cadre of career soldiers.

Businesses do not build around the military's recruiting-training model. And why should they? Few increase their headcounts or experience personnel turnovers of more than 10 percent per year. The Fortune 1000 has not increased net headcount for many years. The challenge for many of the world's largest companies is not scaling *up*, but scaling *back* on the number of full-time employees. This is what makes a company like eBay unique and interesting. Relative to its size, it has had to bring on-board many new people, get them properly trained in their assignments, and imbue them with the culture that its founders intended. Many key employees, such as Senior Vice President of Marketing and International Brian Swette, a former Pepsi-Cola executive, were recruited from traditional corporate cultures and had no background in e-commerce. None had experience in dealing with genuine user communities.

eBay had 135 employees at the beginning of 1999. It added 60 more during that quarter and planned to add 100 or so more in the second quarter—more than doubling total headcount in six months. Add to these the 300 employees of companies acquired from rapid-fire acquisitions and you have a major scale-up in human resources. A quick scan of the company jobs page in early April 2000 indicated 126 more positions waiting to be filled, almost all in San Jose, Salt Lake City, and San Francisco.

Recognizing the danger that the company's original culture could dissipate, Whitman began a practice of meeting with a different group of newly hired employees every Monday morning. During these meetings she describes the company's values and its expectations of them. These new employees are also given opportunities to meet hardcore eBay users during Voice of the Customer Day. As described in Chapter 3, Voice of the Customer Day brings groups of active users into the San Jose headquarters each week for focus sessions and meetings with employees. One purpose of this practice is to inculcate new hires with community esprit and the values intended by founder Omidyar.

The possibility that the management team will stumble on the human resource side of company building—recruiting, training, motivating, and instilling new hires with eBay values and a sense of common purpose—is a real risk, and one generally overlooked by investors and analysts.

■ A DIFFERENT KIND OF MANAGEMENT?

eBay's working environment and the issues it faces in dealing with rapid growth are not entirely unique. Many other Internet businesses face the same challenges, which raises the question: Is there a formula for success in managing Internet businesses?

Lots of people are trying to determine what it takes to run a dot-com company—would-be migrants from the old economy in particular. The old management principles of planning, organizing, motivating, and controlling (POMC) were developed over most of the past century. And though new generations of business students continue to be lectured on the universality of these principles, they now seem quaint relics of an earlier age, most applicable to the large, hierarchical organizations that have become less and less relevant. Most dot-coms are so small, in terms of employee headcounts, that one wonders if traditional POMC principles are even applicable. After all, high-growth start-ups in traditional commerce have never adhered to them, so why would we expect to find them at work in the Internet economy?

The dot-com world is so new that little research has been done to identify its unique management requirements. One study, however, deserves consideration. In mid- to late 1999 Lynne M. H. Rosansky and Russell Reynolds

Associates (RRA) conducted interviews with senior executives at 18 dot-com companies—including a number of the major players. Their goal was to identify the characteristics associated with successful dot-com managers. As summarized on the Russell Reynolds Web site, and later reported in the *Industry Standard,* e-commerce managers exhibited a unique set of characteristics. In addition to the usual business skills, functional expertise, and leadership qualities, top Internet executives also have the following qualities and characteristics:

Recognize opportunity—"CarpeDiem.com." Executives with Web DNA seize the day and jump on business concepts, new business models, innovative operating tools and make bold moves to further their business with a minimum of delay.

Radiate vision. Evangelical in projecting their beliefs about their business, these executives stay focused and make it their priority to communicate their vision persistently to the entire organization.

80/20 mindset. Executives with Web DNA know that it's better to be 80 percent right today than 100 percent right tomorrow. In the face of incomplete information, they can draw on experience and insight to fill in the blanks.

Get the "right stuff" done. Persistently seeking value from all activity, they keep themselves from getting distracted into tangential tasks with little pay-off.

Organizational improvisers. Developing variations of standard business and organizational models, these leaders build and maintain fluid organizations responsive to customer needs and competitor moves. The right people are in the right place to respond swiftly and effectively.

Learning-obsessed. Constantly in the feedback loop and incorporating significant new information, successful Internet executives continually seek data to assess business models, evaluate trends and learn—and they hold themselves to high personal standards of continual self-examination and self-improvement.[13]

These characteristics of successful dot-com managers underscore the great divide between the management in the online world and in large traditional corporations. Let's consider what appear to be the two most important of these characteristics: opportunity seeking, and the 80/20 mindset.

➤ Opportunity Seeking

Time, attention, resources, and organization for the dot-com are focused on finding and responding to opportunities. It is a key activity. Like big amoebae, these companies sense and quickly respond to external stimuli, expand their cell boundaries in the direction of nutrient sources, and draw back from areas that are fallow. Opportunity seeking in the traditional corporate world, in contrast, involves only a small percentage of personnel—mostly research and development (R&D) personnel and a few intrepid marketing types. The larger army of employees—high and low—is dedicated to keeping the machinery of the enterprise operating smoothly. And it is managed with that in mind.

➤ 80/20 Mindset

Both types of organizations, however, follow the same process in dealing with opportunities, a process that R&D people call the *fuzzy front end* of innovation. Figure 5.1 shows a graphic illustration of that process, which, in a large organization, generally involves three sets of partici-

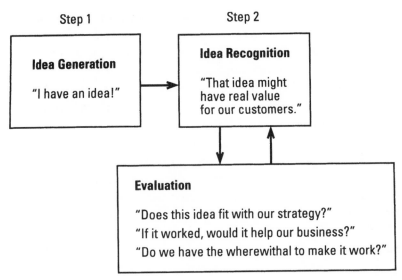

Figure 5.1 The fuzzy front end of the innovation process.
(*From Lee A. Sage,* Winning the Innovation Race [*New York: John Wiley & Sons, 2000*],
p. 14. Reproduced with permission.)

pants: (1) an individual with an innovative idea, (2)
another person (usually an R&D manager) who recognizes the business potential of the idea, and (3) a larger
group of technical and business managers who must evaluate the idea and determine if it deserves formal consideration for funding. The fuzzy front end is generally
informal and moves ideas along quickly. In the large corporation, however, any idea that passes through this front
end successfully enters a second process designed to test
its merits as it develops. This second process—generally
organized as a series of *stage gates*—evaluates and eliminates bad ideas before they absorb too many investment
dollars. Every stage of the innovative idea's development
ends at a gate where its technical or business validity is
reexamined. Each gate is used as an opportunity to send
the idea back for more development, fund its next stage of
development, or kill it entirely.

Needless to say, the stage-gate process can be long and tortuous. And its primary purpose is to reduce the risk of making heavy investments in unworthy projects by eliminating uncertainty. This stands in sharp contrast to the 80/20 mindset identified by the Rosansky RRA study. Dot-com managers recognize what risk-taking investors have understood for a very long time: If you delay until you've reduced most or all the uncertainty in a decision, the opportunity will have slipped through your fingers.

Perhaps without making the calculation, these managers understand intuitively that the cost of a mistake is much less than the cost of a missed opportunity. eBay's case makes the point. The wealth created by its first-mover advantage has vastly exceeded whatever losses Omidyar and Skoll would have incurred back in 1995 had their person-to-person auction concept failed to fly. It was clearly better to jump into the new game as early as possible, and to figure out the game as it revealed itself. This seems to be the case with the online experience in general.

The characteristics described by Rosansky and RRA as correlating with managerial success in e-commerce are surely useful as growing dot-com companies recruit CEOs, marketers, and other executives. However, these characteristics could just as well describe the keys to success for managers in *any* small, entrepreneurial company—online or off. And it is important to remember that all successful dot-coms—including those with enormous market capitalizations and brand names—are small in terms of employee headcounts. eBay, Excite, Webvan, and Buy.com each employ less than 500 people. Even industry giants like Yahoo!, e-Trade, and Amazon have payrolls of only 1,000 to 2,500 people.

These are small, entrepreneurial companies that through the alchemy of the Internet manage to produce huge economic activities. And they continue to *act* like entrepreneurs. But these companies won't remain small forever. As they grow and hire managers adept at keeping the machinery running smoothly, is there is a real danger that they will begin to resemble slower, more deliberate plodders? During the first quarter of 2000, Amazon recruited many senior executives from traditional Fortune 1000 companies—people experienced in managing large-scale enterprises. Priceline did the same. What will happen when the kids let the adults take over? Will the fast, focused Internet bombshells of today begin to resemble the behemoths of the Fortune 1000—with paneled offices for bigwigs, plodding committees, serial problem solving, operational silos, and (God forbid) dress codes?

That's the big unanswered question.

Dot-coms have the potential to remain fast and focused to the extent that their core value-adding functions are scalable without adding layers and their other functions can be outsourced. eBay is potentially one of these.

➤ The Direction of Talent Migration

In the initial stage of the Internet economy, American business experienced a one-way migration of executive and technical talent from the Fortune 1000 and top-tier business schools to the dot-com companies of the new economy. The growing Internet companies needed people with deep experience in managing processes and people, and they could offer the financial incentives needed to lure them: salaries *plus* stock options that offered every expectation of sudden and substantial wealth. The new economy was *hot*.

In contrast, the blue-chip leaders of the old economy were unable in almost every case to recruit the experienced Internet executives they needed to create online ventures of their own. They had nothing to offer. Pay equity within their executive ranks prohibited them from offering huge salaries. And their stock option plans were comparatively uninviting. Who wanted to get rich the old-fashioned way, through years of work and very gradual wealth accumulation when a faster track was available?

In the second stage of the Internet revolution, traditional companies are setting up their own Internet operations in the face of difficult recruiting problems. They need to lure competent and experienced talent from the gold fields of Silicon Valley and other hot spots to the organizations that so many were glad to leave behind. It's not an easy sell, but they are learning how to do it.

Per RRA's Tuck Rickards, traditional companies that succeed in recruiting Internet talent are setting up their operations to look like Internet companies, with equity upside opportunities and decision-making autonomy. Chase.com with its separate equity base, physical separation from the mother ship, and its no-ties, no-suits environment, is just one example. Old-line consulting companies like McKinsey are doing the same. It's still a hard sell, but they are making some progress in attracting Internet talent to corporate America.

Chapter

6

Strategic Evolution

■ MORE AND MORE USERS ■ STRENGTHENING THE BRAND
■ BROADENING THE PLATFORM ■ ENHANCING FEATURES
AND FUNCTIONALITY ■ NO TIME TO CONSOLIDATE
■ A KEY LESSON

One of the big differences between entrepreneurial companies and most lumbering corporate behemoths is how they approach opportunities. When a bright person inside a big corporation sees a juicy opportunity, he or she sets off a long train of activities that aims to measure the potential of the opportunity and analyze its details. Different scenarios of how the opportunity might unfold are sketched out, and probabilities are assigned to each. Lots of attention is given to what can go wrong. Sales and costs are projected (guessed at) over a period of several years. Elaborate pro forma financial statements are developed to determine future cash flows. Present value and internal rate of return are calculated.

Projects that don't meet corporation return hurdles get scratched. The numbers—and the many assumptions on which they are based—are debated at length. Someone in authority usually suggests that the matter needs more study. And so it goes around the circle once more. Everything in this routine is designed for one purpose: to reduce risk. The more that's known, the fewer the uncertainties, and the lower the chance of screwing up. And if the bright new idea threatens any of the corporation's existing products or services, it may be undermined by all the people who benefit from the status quo.

Entrepreneurs have a very different approach to opportunities. They look, they check, and they jump in, even when hundreds of questions remain to be answered. How will the market develop? Who else might get into this business? What are the customer requirements, and how will those requirements change? How will we fund the business if growth takes off? Entrepreneurs understand that many of these questions cannot be reliably answered. As described in the previous chapter, they figure that they'll learn and adapt as they move forward. In any case, the issues that seem important today may not be the ones that matter a year or two down the road. In a nutshell: Entrepreneurs are less concerned with certainty than with getting into the game quickly and learning how to play. This is one of the important reasons that *almost all* major innovations in technology and business models are pioneered by small start-ups instead of major corporations.

In the online world, many of the notable successes have been scored by people who had *no clue* that their new ventures would be big or commercially successful. Take David Filo and Jerry Yang, the two Stanford computer science graduate students who founded Yahoo! They had no long-term strategic plan, no pro formas, no nothing. There was no market worth measuring. Their now-immense business began as a personal pastime in which they bookmarked lists of interesting Web sites on Mosaic, an early browser, and shared them with others on their own site. Now these guys are billionaires. Amazon's Jeff Bezos provides a similar example. Bezos professes to be as surprised as anyone with the success of his online bookselling idea and its subsequent evolutions. Pierre Omidyar has said essentially the same about his experience with eBay. He had no clear idea about how things would develop.

In each of these cases, long-term strategies only emerged in evolutionary ways in response to challenges and newfound opportunities. Pierre Omidyar had no thought of acquiring a live auction house like Butterfield & Butterfield. Nor was there a plan to open regional eBay auctions, which have now grown in number to 57. Nor had zShops or auctions been part of Jeff Bezo's plan. These things happened incrementally, through a process of learning and opportunistic experimentation.

Incremental strategic evolution could easily have dissipated the energy and resources of these companies if they had chased after every good opportunity. Successful Internet companies have lots of opportunities thrown at them, and getting sidetracked is a constant danger. Some might say that Amazon has already fallen victim to this problem. Opportunistic behavior at eBay, however, has been bounded by two things: a clear mission to be the world's largest person-to-person online auction company, and a focused strategy with five key elements:

- Expanding the user base
- Strengthening the eBay brand
- Broadening the trading platform by increasing product categories and promoting new ones
- Fostering community affinity
- Enhancing site features and functionality

Though the company is highly responsive to the threats and opportunities that it encounters from week to week, its clear sense of purpose and focused strategy reduce the chance that it will run off the tracks. With the exception of community affinity, which has been described at length earlier, we will examine the key elements of eBay's strategy in the following sections of this chapter.

■ MORE AND MORE USERS

During the three-year period ending in December 1999, the number of registered eBay users skyrocketed from 41,000 to 10 million. That's an annual compound growth rate of 535 percent. Few companies have expanded at such a pace.

Because "registered users" includes everyone who has ever registered to trade on the site, we should accept these figures with some skepticism. After all, some users have probably died. A certain percentage will have gotten bored with the site and moved on. And at least a few (mostly people living in southern California) have surely fallen victim to alien abductions, never to trade again. So what's the number of *active* users? Half the official count? One-third? If the company knows, it isn't telling. Nor is it important to know because gross merchandise sales are what really matter, and these have grown at an even *higher* rate (627 percent per year) over the same period.

These are amazing numbers. Even the best of the old-economy companies like Boeing, 3M, and Merck must gasp when they see a growth rate like this reported in the paper. But eBay's executives must also shudder when they see them. Given the expectations built into eBay's stock price, its management cannot allow the pace of growth to slacken. But where will the new users come from? The answer is threefold:

- *Continued penetration of the North American market.* Roughly half of all adults in the United States and Canada had access to the Internet in 1999. Millions more will be added to the ranks in each of the coming years. At the same time, with 10 million registered users in 1999, 80 percent of current Internet users were unregistered. The company hopes to gain a greater share of this untapped market.

- *Bringing in the rest of the world.* Non-U.S. buyers have bought and sold on eBay since its earliest days, but through 1998, these accounted for only a tiny fraction of gross merchandise sales. Customs duties, inspections, shipping problems, and language and currency issues have stood in the way. Since the U.S. population represents less than 6 percent of the global village, the largest untapped source of new users is outside English-speaking North America. In 1999, the company undertook major offshore initiatives, setting up eBay trading sites to cover Great Britain, Germany, Australia, and Japan.[1] It aims to expand to other locations in the months and years ahead.

- *Bringing in different user groups.* In the beginning, eBay had been strictly a person-to-person operation. Over time, this expanded to include small-dealer-to-person trading, a group that now dominates volume selling. All indicators, however, point to business-to-business trading as the much larger venue in the future. Just a month before this manuscript went into production, eBay announced a new site within its site, dubbed Business Exchange, dedicated to small merchants trading with each other. This is a new and potentially large source of users—best of all, they will be trading workstations and drill presses, not low-priced Beanie Babies. More on this later.

■ STRENGTHENING THE BRAND

The concept of the *brand* has important competitive implications in traditional consumer commerce. David Aaker's widely read book on brand management defines a *brand* as "a distinguishing name and/or symbol (such as a logo, trademark, or package design) intended to identify the goods or services of either one seller or a group of sellers, and to differentiate those goods or services from those of competitors."[2]

A powerful and highly recognized brand name generally results in greater unit sales and allows the seller to charge a premium over "off-brand" competitors. Rightly or wrongly, consumers associate brand names with higher quality or the right choice. When confronted with perplexing choices, or many choices, they often default to names they know—familiar brands.

Powerful brand names command shelf space unavailable to others. For example, grocers will always make space on their crowded shelves for Bounty paper towels, Kellogg's corn flakes, and Campbell's soups. They are the brands most asked for by customers. Lesser brands must fight among themselves for the remaining space.

Powerful brands can also open adjacent markets when marketers and product developers work together to create *brand extensions* such as Starbucks coffee ice cream, Folger's decaffeinated coffee, or Ritz Bits crackers. All of these products have surrounded themselves in the positive aura of the original branded product, and in so doing have improved their odds of success in new markets. Is it surprising, then, that corporations spend royally to establish and sustain their brands, and to protect them from encroachment?

The principles of brand management are widely understood and applied in the traditional economy. However, their application in e-commerce is less appreciated, even though the need for branding is often as compelling. Phil Carpenter, who has written the first complete study of e-commerce branding, makes a powerful case for brand development. With the number of Web sites exploding, he says, it's easy to get lost in the clutter:

> Imagine that you're walking down the aisle of the local grocery store on your weekly shopping run. As you reach for the laundry detergent, you're surprised to see the range of options in front of you suddenly double. You attempt to grab the fabric softener. The number of brands on the shelf dou-

bles—then triples—in about thirty seconds. Choice rapidly becomes overwhelming.[3]

E-businesses can stand out from the clutter, according to Carpenter, through effective branding. And he makes a case for a number of *best practices* found in the companies he studied:

- Focus on building brand awareness through online and offline advertising, good public relations, and *guerrilla marketing* ploys.
- Cultivate customer commitment through programs that build loyalty.
- Forge strong distribution and content alliances.
- Move early and fast—and keep the category's evolution at a high pace.
- Develop an intimate knowledge of market and customer.
- Cultivate a reputation for excellence—for example, with a site design that is highly functional, clear, consistent, and fast.
- Deliver outstanding value.

The arrival of Meg Whitman in early 1998 marked a watershed in the effort to build brand recognition at eBay. The company's early growth relied strictly on word of mouth. But as an old hand at consumer product marketing, Whitman made branding one of her first initiatives. In a series of meetings with the senior management team, she broke the problem into two parts. The first was clarifying what eBay stood for. In their judgment, it was a *personal* trading community where users could buy and sell *almost anything*. This definition set it apart from most existing auction competitors and the several that eventually followed. All market communications now reflect this unequivocal definition.

Part two of Whitman's branding exercise came directly from Marketing 101: market segmentation. The user community was analyzed in terms of user segments. Serious collectors and small dealers were identified as the heaviest site users. These individuals and the people who sold to them accounted for 80 percent of total eBay revenues even though they represented only 20 percent of registered users. Based on this knowledge, the company decided to concentrate its marketing and brand-building resources on them. This meant a major reduction in broadband advertising, such as on Web portal sites, and more aggressive spending on the many niche publications read by serious collectors. The company also exhibited at collector trade shows (over 90 in 1998 alone).[4] At the same time, it began the development of beneficial programs for heavy users, such as the PowerSellers program.

The company also began to reinforce its brand within the existing eBay community through marketing programs on the eBay Web site, a commercial magazine (*eBay*), and through the distribution of eBay-branded merchandise.

➤ The AOL Connection

eBay's boldest and most costly effort of gaining greater name recognition began in August 1998, when it entered into a three-year marketing deal with America Online (AOL). Under the terms of this relationship, AOL would feature eBay as its preferred provider of person-to-person trading services in its classifieds and interest areas. In addition, an eBay link would appear on the AOL home page, a portal for some 64 million subscribers. This three-year deal was priced at $12 million.

In March 1999, the term of the relationship was extended by an additional year, and its scope was expanded to include an eBay presence on AOL's other properties: Digital Cities, ICQ, CompuServe, and Netscape. The total cost of this amended agreement was a cool $75 million.

➤ eBay Meets Disney

February 8, 2000, was not a good day to make a major announcement. eBay and several other major Internet sites were frozen with denial-of-service attacks. Nevertheless, it was the day on which eBay officials chose to announce a four-year agreement with GO.com, a network of the Walt Disney Company's Web sites, which included ABC.com, ESPN.com, and Disney.com. Under this agreement, eBay and GO.com would work together to develop a *cobranded* site promoted by the GO.com network, an Internet portal with millions of users, and comarketed with Disney throughout the latter's offline channels, which included ABC television and radio networks, ESPN's cable network, Disney Channel, and the Disney catalog and theme parks.

This new relationship served two important purposes for eBay: brand recognition and a powerful magnet for attracting new users. Disney is one of the world's most recognized brands and, significantly, one associated with fun and family-friendly activities (certain movies distributed by its film subsidiary notwithstanding). Association with the world of Disney and its far-reaching channels of communication was certain to create new legions of auction buyers and sellers. Furthermore, Disney memorabilia was already trading fast and furious on eBay, with almost 30,000 such items listed on any given day. According to the company's announcement board: "It has been our experience that highly publicized unique items (similar to the ones that Disney might be selling) will attract many new members to eBay. In fact, these Disney, ABC and ESPN related items, will act as a magnet for attracting Disney, ABC/entertainment and ESPN/sports enthusiasts to eBay, and expanding the market for the whole eBay community."

Disney's GO.com had made a furtive effort to enter the online auction business only four months earlier, but as a latecomer, had gotten almost nowhere. Under the terms of the agreement, the two enterprises would collaborate in developing a cobranded auction site identified as ebay.go.com. Auctions listed on this new site, which went online in May 2000, would be co-listed on other Disney Web sites, including Disney.com, ESPN.com and ABC.com. eBay's announcement raised the expectation that the new site would showcase unique and exclusive products and memorabilia from Walt Disney Studios, Disney theme parks, ESPN cable networks, and ABC television.

"We are very excited about this relationship," Meg Whitman told the business press. "We believe that it will be extremely beneficial for the whole eBay community—for the host of new members and items it will bring to the eBay world, and just as importantly, for the promotion it will bring eBay in the world of Disney."

■ BROADENING THE PLATFORM

eBay had a good head start in the race to acquire auction users. But with new competitors jumping into the game every month, its managers knew that they would suffer defections and fail to capture new market territory if they did not make their site progressively bigger, better, and more varied. Their response was a two-pronged strategy:

- Introduce new higher-priced product categories.
- Extend the service geographically.

eBay aimed to head upstream, into higher-priced categories of antiques, art, and collectibles. The acquisition of Butterfield & Butterfield, an old-line San Francisco–based auction house, with $260 million in eBay stock served that purpose. So, too, did the acquisition of Kruse International, a brand name in the field of collector-quality automobiles. Kruse participated in some 40 classic car auctions each year and enjoyed relationships with collectors and classic car dealers worldwide.

Moving into higher-priced item categories makes perfect business sense. Because few eBay infrastructure and operating expenses vary with the price of items sold at auction, the higher gross sales revenues produced by collector-quality artworks, automobiles, and similar items result in much higher operating profits. For example, the auction of a single $500 Venetian glass vase produces the same operating profits as eleven $40 celebrity autographs. And the sale of a high-priced item does not put any more strain on the electronic infrastructure than one that sells for a few dollars.

➤ Testing New Ideas in Real Time

As it introduces new categories, site features, and policies, eBay uses its direct digital connection to users to gain rapid feedback. Feedback is gained through live discussions and instant customer surveys. It listens to reactions to those items and makes changes accordingly. Some of the site's best ideas—like the current feedback profiles—were produced in this way.

➤ On to Autos

While the Butterfield and Kruse acquisitions extended the company's reach into higher-priced collectibles, two subsequent strategic relationships gave the company a window into another category of high-priced goods, but one that was huge by comparison: the used auto market.

eBay's window into this huge trade came through a negotiated deal with AutoTrade.com, which, at the time, was the world's largest used-car marketplace. In the typical month, 5 million unique visitors click onto the Auto-Trade site to view the wheels and sheet metal listed by more than 40,000 participating auto dealers and 250,000 private sellers. Under the terms of their agreement, the two companies would cobrand a site.

The eBay-AutoTrade deal was a powerful supplement to the site's August 1999 deal with CarClub.com, which provided registered users with direct access to CarClub's vehicle inspection and warranty service. Under this arrangement, users who wanted to buy or sell a vehicle on an eBay auction would be able to request a comprehensive inspection of the car from CarClub's nationwide network of certified technicians. Vehicles that passed the inspection were eligible for CarClub's comprehensive used-car protection plan, which, for a fee, provided mechanical coverage similar to that of new car's manufacturer's warranties. The motivation for this alliance was to neutralize the very real concern that every used-car purchaser has about unseen defects and thereby facilitate a more active market in these higher-priced items.

➤ Regional eBays

Creating higher traffic in higher-priced categories, such as automobiles, furniture, clothes washers, and dryers, was clearly in eBay's interest, but shipping and handling problems with these categories made them much more challenging for users than trading baseball cards and record collections. These products traditionally had

HERE COMES THE NADA

Bowing to concerns that its member dealers would see their sales wither under a barrage of Internet-based car-selling innovations, the National Automobile Dealers Association (NADA) decided to fight fire with fire. In March 2000, the NADA announced plans to launch its own car-shopping site, and hoped that most of its 19,500 U.S. dealers would join in. The expectation was that the site's database would eventually list some 500,000 vehicles on its members' lots, along with dealer invoice prices (something dealers had long resisted revealing) and the NADA's highly regarded used-car pricing data.

been exchanged through local or regional classified ads for this reason. Always eager to find an online analog to a traditional commercial practice, eBay strategists latched onto the idea of creating regional online auction sites. These sites listed items both on the All-eBay site and on single metropolitan area sites, such as eBay Chicago. By January 2000, the company was operating 57 regional sites encompassing the largest markets in the United States.

Regional sites have proven beneficial for both buyers and sellers. Buyers can often arrange to physically inspect their purchases before settling, and they stand to save on shipping time and expense by picking up the items they purchase. Sellers, on the other hand, avoid packing and shipping chores by specifying pickup only.

➤ The Business-to-Business Bombshell

When interviewed in February 2000, eBay board director Bob Kagle indicated that the company was keeping its options open on strategic moves outside its traditional person-to-person territory. No less than a month later, the company exercised that option, announcing the launch of the Business Exchange, a new area of the site dedicated to small business auction trading. "The Business Exchange pulls together business-related categories (like computers, video editing equipment and industrial equipment) from different areas of eBay and puts them in one location," a company press release proclaimed. "It also features a series of shortcuts to business-related searches where buyers can click directly to find what they're looking for." A quick tour of the Business Exchange indicated that over 60,000 items had already been shifted to that part of the site: power tools, computer equipment, office furniture, toner cartridges, and dozens of other categories.

A fair amount of small-business-to-business trading had always taken place on the site, but the launch of Business Exchange aimed to expand the scope of this activity.

The clear aim was to give eBay a toehold in a huge and growing segment of e-commerce, the total volume of which is projected to dwarf consumer activity in the years ahead. Though analysts did not forecast any near-term profit improvements attributable to the Business Exchange, the long-term view was highly positive. "Everybody in the B2B world looks at eBay as the progenitor of the whole model," Keenan Vision financial analyst Vernon Keenan told the *New York Times* when the plan first went public. "eBay is clearly the 500-pound gorilla in Internet exchange transactions today."[5]

■ ENHANCING FEATURES AND FUNCTIONALITY

One of the most obvious lessons that every online retailer has had to learn is the importance of site functionality and value-adding features. Presentations have to be clear, information must be right to the point, every feature must be easy to access, and site navigation should be intuitively obvious. Any novice who stumbles onto the site should be able to find what he or she wants and order it with the least amount of effort. Fast, convenient, trouble-free: These are supposed to be the virtues of buying online.

A site also benefits to the extent that its features add real value (e.g., links to currency conversions on foreign travel sites, and book reviews on Amazon) or make the visitor's interactions with the site trouble-free (e.g., a feature that recognizes regular users and processes transactions without asking them to repeat their credit-card numbers and mailing addresses).

Auction sites like eBay must go another step further—a very big step further. They must make it as easy and straightforward as possible for two very different groups, buyers and sellers, to transact a much more complex set of activities.

Bidding and buying on eBay has always been easy. You

find your favorite thing, check out the reputation of the seller through the Feedback system rating, and make your bid. You can either check in periodically to observe the progress of the auction and make higher bids if necessary, or you can tell eBay to increase your bids incrementally as needed up to a stated amount. If yours is the winning bid, the seller lets you know, and tells you where to send the check. Bingo. The only challenge for the buyer is keeping track of several auctions in which he or she is a participant, but the site's handy My eBay feature handles this chore easily.

Selling has always been substantially more difficult. Lots of things have to be learned from scratch, such as listing the item and writing a complete and compelling description (and perhaps using HTML to enhance its appearance). If a photograph is appropriate (and they are in most cases), that photo must be digitized, uploaded to a hosting site, and linked to the auction. The seller must also make a number of strategic decisions, often without the guidance of empirical information:

- How many days should the auction be posted?
- What opening minimum bid should be set?
- Should a reserve price be used? Reserves tend to drive away bargain-hunting bidders.
- When is the ideal time for the auction to end? Because so much bidding takes place in the final hours of a scheduled auction, it might not be smart to end at a time when most people are sleeping or at work.

Experienced sellers get a feel for these questions, but certainty is elusive.

Once the auction begins, the seller may have to answer e-mail requests for more information from potential bidders. And once the auction is consummated, the seller is responsible for contacting the winning bidder via e-mail and arranging payment and shipping.

Learning how to do each of these tasks for the first time requires substantial time and effort—even if you have one of the several available books on how to buy and sell on eBay on your desk. Once you've been through the drill two or three times, little learning effort remains. However, the routine chores do, and these are impediments to auction activity—the source of eBay's revenues.

The company has incrementally attacked the barriers to auction trading over the years, spending $4.6 million and $23.7 million in 1998 and 1999, respectively, on product developments aimed at site enhancement and value-adding features. The various SafeHarbor features such as the Feedback Forum, the Mister Lister bulk-listing tool, help boards, and My eBay, which allows a user to track multiple auctions simultaneously, fall into this category. Generally, the most important chore-reducing features have been added through arrangements with partner firms or third-party suppliers such as iEscrow, iShip, Mailbox Etc., and Wells Fargo's Billpoint credit-card arrangement.

The company has indicated that it will continue to pursue more seamless functionality on its site. And it has a long way to go. Like competing sites, it has a gerry-rigged feel to it, with lots of loosely connected elements brought together. This is a symptom of the incremental development common to many new product areas, both traditional and online. eBay will most likely not introduce a major makeover of its site. Doing so could confuse and annoy millions of users who have grown accustomed to the current site, and who have learned its idiosyncrasies. Some daily newspapers have learned this lesson the hard way. In giving their papers a new look, they offended the very customers they hoped to please. In all likelihood, eBay will continue on its current course of making many small, little-noticed changes and improvements to its site.

The company gives users opportunities to comment about or push back against newly introduced site features via a discussion board. This direct and rapid feedback makes it possible to retract or refine changes or new features that rub users the wrong way or could stand improving. A quick review of comments left on the new-feature discussion board indicates that users are not shy about sounding off when they believe that one of the company's little innovations is either cutting into their trade or making their interactions with the site more difficult.

> Am I the only one that thinks the "Watch This Item" link in auctions is driving sellers to the poorhouse? Geez . . . Bidding is bad enough without encouraging bidders NOT to bid.
>
> . . . .
>
> I believe the Watch feature has hurt all our auctions. I started using counter on all my auctions when the watch feature came on line . . . it's so depressing to see the count with NO Bids . . . I do have traffic in all my auctions with no bids! Has anyone tried using the watch on something you would like?
>
> . . . .
>
> Ever since the reserve fee went into effect the whole market has slow'd down. I hear—still—a lot of complaints from other local sellers that feels that the reserve fee deal has hurt their income.
>
> . . . .
>
> I can't support your theory right now, sorry. This time of the year always falls into a slump. Taxes

Though not scientific, rapid feedback like this can help the company fine-tune the features and functionality of its site—assuming that management takes feedback seriously.

■ NO TIME TO CONSOLIDATE

The strategy just described seems driven by two irresistible forces. The first is the natural business impulse to capture as much of the new, unoccupied e-commerce terrain as possible, and as *quickly* as possible. In this it is reminiscent of the Oklahoma land rush in nineteenth-century America. Once that new territory was declared open for settlement by the U.S. government, the rush was on, with every farmer and rancher galloping off to stake a claim to as much of the best land as possible. Dot-com companies are doing something very similar—and why not? The cost of this strategy is extremely low. Unlike the cell-phone companies that attempted to play the same strategy a decade earlier, eBay and other dot-coms don't have to give away expensive telephones or several months of free services. Scaling-up costs are high, but eBay is already turning a profit. The more business, the more profits. And if acquisitions are needed to pave the way, the company has plenty of high-priced treasury stock in the vault to finance those deals with little out-of-pocket cost.

Because holding occupied terrain is always easier than wrestling it away from someone else, this strategy makes sense. Further, it supports the positive network effect that eBay as a first mover in person-to-person auctions already enjoys. More buyers and sellers coming to the site give it an even stronger gravitational pull. The downside of this land grab approach, however, is twofold:

- The company could lose its focus and spread its resources too thinly across an expanding universe of categories and users.
- The sense of community on which eBay depends for customer loyalty and site integrity could disintegrate.

The second driver of eBay's strategy is its stratospheric stock price, which in late 1999 and early 2000 periodically spilled into $200-per-share territory (presplit). The primary thing supporting that lofty price, in the absence of substantial profits, is the stock market's expectation of continued geometric growth in numbers of users and revenues. Even a whiff of slackening growth could cause investors to stampede toward the exits, sending confidence in the company and its value into steep decline.

Given this growth imperative, the company must add new legions to its user ranks each and every quarter. As Meg Whitman told interviewers, "It's all about the battle for new consumers. That's why we have to grow faster than our competitors. We have to get people to come to eBay first."[6] And it must keep those customers and keep them trading.

Only time will tell if eBay's five-pronged strategy will sustain the growth its investors expect and demand. From the vantage point of early spring 2000, the signs appear promising. There are still opportunities aplenty for alliances with other powerful Internet sites, and the company's exploitation of high-end goods traffic has only just begun. But life in e-commerce is filled with surprises.

■ A KEY LESSON

The key lesson for managers in this examination of eBay strategy is the virtue of having (1) an unambiguous mission that employees from top to bottom understand, and (2) a focused strategy for pursuing that mission. In the absence of either of these, this company could easily run off the rails in an effort to keep the growth engine going.

Few companies have more growth opportunities than eBay. For the master of the person-to-person auction world, even bigger opportunities are visible in business-to-business auctions. Why not go after these? Think, too, of the 1½ million people who hit the eBay site each day; these people make most of their other purchases through fixed-price venues, both on and off the Web. So why not offer an eBay version of Amazon's zShops to these many visitors? How about banner ads for life insurance sales and other products and sites?

Opportunities for vertical integration and for investments in related business are also available. Instead of paying Exodus and AboveNet for Web-hosting services, why not acquire one of them? Both companies are leaders in an industry that will grow at the same explosive pace as the Internet itself. Isn't diversification good?

By virtue of its heady stock price, eBay has the financial muscle to buy into any bright idea it trips over. And that's the danger: eBay's management team includes many bright people, but their collective experience in managing strategic growth is not very deep. They could easily make a big mistake—chasing off in a new direction or going on an acquisition binge. Here, consensus on the eBay mission and adherence to the five-pronged strategy provide a measure of protection against serious error.

Your company is unlikely to ever grow at eBay's blazing pace. Nor is it likely to see as many growth opportunities. Nevertheless, a clear and unambiguous mission, and a strategic framework for pursuing that mission, can help you and your managers maximize its potential.

Chapter 7

Contraband, Blackouts, and Weird Stuff

■ STRICTLY ILLEGAL ■ REALLY TACKY STUFF
■ OUTAGES—DOWN BUT NOT OUT
■ GROWING PAINS WILL GO AWAY

Though I've never met him, my guess is that eBay Communications Vice President Kevin Pursglove is either the most blessed or most cursed public relations guy in corporate America. On one hand, Pursglove works for one of the Internet's primo companies, which probably pays him handsomely. And he doesn't, like many corporate spokespersons, have to explain to press people how his bosses are closing down a plant and laying off thousands of hapless employees the day before Christmas. On the other hand, as he drives off to work each morning, Pursglove has no idea what strange events he will have to explain to the public. And these keep him pretty busy.

What will it be today? he must ask himself as he maneuvers into the company parking lot. Charles Manson auctioning "Lunch with a Killer—bring your own plastic tray?" A chance to bid on quality time with a porn star? A fault line opening under the South Bay area, swallowing up the company's servers?

Life in the person-to-person auction world is full of surprises. Some events create headlines that bring lots of positive attention to the eBay site, advancing the company's goal of brand recognition—and at no cost. For example, when Peter de Jager, a Canada-based Y2K consultant, listed his Year2000.com Internet address in the closing days of 1999 with a minimum bid of $1 million, it created enormously positive media attention, and plenty of people heard the eBay name for the first time. It also brought in a winning bid of $10 million on New Year's Day for de Jager. But for every auction like de Jager's another casts a cloud. Consider just a few of the high-profile hoaxes that have been perpetrated on the eBay site over the past two years: auctions involving a guided missile, a young man's virginity, 200 pounds of cocaine (minimum bid, $2 million), a human kidney, a human testicle, and at least three babies. Each generated nationwide publicity through stories carried on National Public Radio and major U.S. newspapers. Was this publicity good or bad for eBay? On the positive side, eBay got some free publicity; on the negative side, its brand name was associated with frivolous and even (in the cases of the kidney and babies) cruel behavior. Add to these hoaxes the reports of fraud and trading in counterfeit or stolen goods. All tarnish the company's name. And then there are the service outages that periodically take down the eBay site. Outages cost the company dearly in revenues and user loyalty.

In this chapter we'll look at some of the illegal activities, service outages, and weird goods that show up on the eBay site. Collectively, these are major potholes in the road to the company's continued success. We'll examine their impact on the company's business, and its attempts to deal with them.

■ STRICTLY ILLEGAL

eBay's vision is to have a site where anybody can trade anything. But some things are strictly illegal, including a few that have turned up on the site. For example, offering the human kidney by auction in September 1999 was contrary to U.S. federal law. This turned out to be a hoax, but it drew lots of attention and many bids—most of them equally fraudulent. Later that month, three men listed 500 pounds of marijuana labeled "Holland's Best." An attached photo showed plastic bags filled with a weedlike substance and three guys purported to be the sellers. By the time site administrators spotted and pulled the listing, it had already solicited seven bids.

People have also attempted to sell securities on the eBay site, an activity contrary to U.S. securities regulations.

Other items have fallen into a legal gray area. There were, for instance, memorabilia of the riots provoked by the World Trade Organization meeting in Seattle, Washington, in late 1999. Within a day of these eruptions, spent rubber bullets, tear gas canisters, and even broken police batons appeared on the eBay site. Unsure as to the legal ownership of these items (were they the property of the Seattle police department?), eBay felt obliged to pull the auctions.

There is also the problem of auctions featuring what turn out to be pirated copies of copyrighted materials, such as computer programs like Office 2000 and various Adobe software products. Following the indictment of two individuals alleged to have sold pirated Adobe software on the eBay site, Adobe's corporate counsel was quoted as saying that "the vast majority of software sold on these sites [i.e., auction sites] is pirated." This threatened to bring down the big legal guns of Microsoft and other software powerhouses. The Interactive Digital Software Association was wearing out the phone line to eBay's counsel on this issue, and the company quickly agreed to collaborate with legitimate rights holders in rooting out counterfeit and pirated items. Actually, eBay and sites like it have some protection from liability under the Digital Millennium Copyright Act of 1998 (DMCA) if their networks are used to trade in these illegal items. Under the terms of the act, site providers cannot be held liable if they are unaware of the illegal status of the item or if they lack the ability to control the trade. More specifically, the DMCA stipulates that online publishers bear responsibility for the content of their sites, while online *venues* (like eBay) do not. One could infer from this that eBay's policy of requiring sellers to take responsibility for the legal status of their items quite deliberately puts the company on the right side of this law. eBay has said countless times that its site is merely a forum for people to post advertisements for items. If it took the other approach—that is, if it attempted to verify the legality of every item placed on the site (an impossible task)—it would probably be liable for any fraudulent items that slipped under its screen. And with hundreds of items being listed for auction every minute on eBay, many would surely slip through. Thus, liability can be avoided by taking *no* responsibility for policing the site, whereas a good-faith attempt to police the site can create a liability. This situation has prompted the company to seek a revision of the DMCA that would exempt companies from liability for illegal items if they *did* screen for them.[1]

Though the number of reports of illegal sales on the eBay site is small, it represents a serious dilemma for the company. On one hand, one or two incidents blown up in the press can tarnish the entire image of the company and its service. The press loves these stories and moves them to page 1, even when no one is damaged, as in the fake kidney auction. One the other hand, coming down hard with stringent rules, intense oversight, and arbitrary *do*s and *don't*s runs counter to the laissez-faire, empowered community that Omidyar and many users have worked so hard to develop.

In the end, board member Howard Schultz (CEO and founder of Starbucks) forced a strategic approach to the issue, framing it as one with the potential to bring the company down. As Meg Whitman recalled in an interview: "I remember discussing the situation with the board and describing all the things we were already doing to

THE COUNTERFEIT PROBLEM

In 1999, the Software and Information Industry Association (SIIA) undertook an extensive review of auctions involving the software of its member companies on various sites. According to the SIIA, which counts 1,200 member firms, this study indicated that 60 percent of the software being auctioned was bogus.

The study found 20 different software products of four member companies being auctioned through 221 separate listings on three different auction sites. SIIA antipiracy specialists determined that 109 of these listed items were illegitimate, 72 were legitimate, and the legitimacy of the remaining 40 could not be determined. (The SIIA excluded the 40 undetermined sales from its calculations of the 60 percent bogus figure.)

Another study by the SIIA, this one released in April 2000, found that 90 percent of the software auctions it surveyed were offering pirated products.

How can a bidder recognize a counterfeit product? According to the SIIA, the bidder should be alert to the following clues:

- Missing manuals, documentation, or licensing agreements

- No product registration card

- A product that comes as a CD only or is labeled "Academic" or "Student Version"

- A product that comes on a CD containing software from other publishers that do not normally collaborate on distribution with the product's publisher

- A price that is simply too good to be true

(Continues)

(Continued)

The magnitude of counterfeit production of leading applications programs is estimated to be about $11 billion per year. Consider just one incident: In the early morning hours of March 6, 1998, police in Baldwin, California, raided a facility identified by a tipster as an underground manufacturer of program knockoffs. In this single raid, more than 17,000 counterfeit copies of Microsoft Office 97 and the Microsoft Windows 95 operating system were confiscated.

address the problem when Howard stopped me and said, 'Meg, it's about the character of the company.' I sat back and thought about his comment and within five days we had changed our entire strategy to be much more proactive."[2] That strategy involved the introduction of protection services for users and more aggressive efforts to identify and pull illegal items.

Today, the company is feeling more and more pressure to take greater responsibility for transactions that take place on its site.

■ REALLY TACKY STUFF

Illegal items have been the least of eBay's problems. When something is illegal, the right course of action is always clear: prohibition. The strange, the distasteful, and the offensive, on the other hand, are more vexing. These have brought the company lots of negative publicity and have forced it in many cases—and against its wishes—to act as censor. Consider the case of the racist Internet address. An anonymous seller listed a racist Internet domain name with a minimum bid requirement of $1 million, prompting more than 20 bids and an angry outburst from the National Association for the Advancement of Colored People, which chided eBay for "selling hate, bigotry, and racial stereotypes." The company pulled the auction, citing its language as a violation of community guidelines.

Another problem area in terms of auction propriety centers on memorabilia associated with criminal events. The appearance of Nazi collectibles on the site is just one of many examples. eBay's Butterfield & Butterfield unit has dealt in these items before, and once attracted a $1-million winning bid for Adolf Hitler's personal phone book. It took the view that such items are historical artifacts to which the public should have access. The Simon Wiesenthal Center thought differently, complaining that auctions of Nazi memorabilia glorify the horrors of the Nazi era. Spokesman Pursglove responded that "Our community has encouraged us from the beginning to be an open venue where people can trade practically anything, and eBay is hesitant to perform the role of censor." Pursglove's position notwithstanding, the company soon came around with a compromise on Nazi material and similar items associated with the Ku Klux Klan and other organizations.

The problem of determining what is and what isn't permissible has plagued eBay from its founding, and it has forced it to develop policies on adult material, liquor, firearms, body parts, human remains, and other categories. Over time, it has developed policies and guidelines for three problematic categories of materials in its user agreement: prohibited, questionable, and potentially infringing. *Prohibited* materials may not be listed on eBay, period, but *questionable* items may be listed under certain conditions. *Potentially infringing* is defined as items that may be "in violation of certain copyrights, trademarks, or other rights."

Adult material is listed as *questionable* in eBay policy, but what does this mean? In the interest of scholarly research, I felt compelled to find the answer. Donning a set of dark glasses to conceal my identity, I ventured into eBay's trashy back alley. Only two gatekeepers protected

> ## EVERYONE'S PROBLEM
>
> The policy problems associated with materials considered offensive or racist by particular groups are not eBay's alone. For example, when *The Protocols of the Learned Elders of Zion* was found in the online databases of Amazon.com and Barnesandnoble.com, the you-know-what hit the fan. A nineteenth-century book written and circulated by the secret police of Czarist Russia, *Protocols* purports to reveal a secret Jewish plan to take over the world. The Anti-Defamation League (ADL) calls it a tool of anti-Semites and in early 2000 wanted it purged from the lists of the two big book e-tailers. Amazon initially resisted, stating through a spokesperson that "We are a book seller, not a book censor." Barnesandnoble took a similar stance.
>
> Eventually, both vendors backpedaled and agreed to post the ADL's statement about the book on their Web sites. In the end, this simply opened the companies to attack from both sides. One customer wrote that she would not buy another book from Amazon until it stopped selling such "hate-mongering" materials. At the same time, the Electronic Frontier Foundation called the policy a mistake and an invitation for other groups to seek similar disclaimers on whatever materials they found offensive.

my innocent eyes from what lay ahead: the usual "are you 18 years old" page (yes, many times over), and another that required my user name, password, and credit-card number. Entering the site I encountered lots of steamy stuff: back issues of Playboy and Hustler; sex toys for men and women; "8000 Nude Celebrity Pictures!"; "Homemade CD—Me and My Latina Girlfriend . . . HOT!!!"; "The Interactive [video] Adventures of Seymour Butts." And page after page more. Like other listings, eBay's adult items are generally accompanied by photographic samples, some of which would make a hooker blush.

Dealing with "offensive" material is difficult for eBay. After all, this company has made a fortune off the fact that one person's trash is another person's treasure. Taking a strong stand on one offensive class of material creates friction among different constituents. In a balkanized age in which many religious, ethnic, racial, or national groups are quick to take offense or claim victimhood, the term *offensive material* can cover a broad territory. If Nazi memorabilia is a no-no, what about Native American artifacts, relics of the slave era, or items relating to the Armenian massacres of the early nineteenth century? Where do you draw the line, especially for collectors? How might families of murder victims feel about these particular eBay auctions:

Ted Bundy serial killer and mass murderer trading card featuring artist rendering and factual text on one of the most notorious serial killer and mass murderers of all time. This card was issued by Eclipse Enterprises (1992). Mint condition set comes in display holder for viewing or storing. Good luck!!

. . . .

Just in case you could not attend the service, here is the prayer card! Has prayer and picture of Christ, along with the death date and name of our friend, stating that he has 'entered into eternal rest.' This card is in Very Good condition. Very weird, and impossible to find! Buyer to pay .75 cents postage.

. . . .

Charles Manson address labels with YOUR name and address on them!! Charles Manson - the man who got a bunch of middle class kids to cut up a bunch of rich people to help start a 'Race War' on your very own labels!! 3 sheets of 30 labels. That's 90 letters to send out to Uncle Charlie at Corcoran Prison!!!

. . . .

A hand written letter by the world's most famous serial killer, Charles Manson, plus an extra note. I'll

THE BIG LIST

As of March 2000, eBay listed the following prohibited, questionable, and potentially infringing items in its user agreement. The meanings of most prohibited, questionable, and potentially infringing categories—with examples—are spelled out in detail on the eBay site.

Prohibited	Questionable	Potentially Infringing
Advertisements	Adults only	Copyrights and
Alcohol	Artifacts	trademarks
Animal and	Food	Faces, names,
wildlife products	Freon	signatures
Bulk e-mail lists	International	Games: Sega,
Counterfeit currency	transactions	Nintendo, Sony
and stamps	Offensive	Imported items
Counterfeit	materials	Key word
items	Police-related	spamming
Countries and	items	Music, movies,
persons	Scanners and	and photos
Drugs and drug	electronics	Promotional items
paraphernalia	equipment	Software
Embargoed items	Tickets	Trademarked items
Firearms	Used clothing	
Fireworks	Used medical	
Government IDs	devices	
and licenses		
Weapons and knives		
Human parts and		
remains		
Postage meters		
Prescription drugs/		
materials		
Tobacco		

(Continues)

TV descramblers
Stocks and other
  securities
Stolen property
Surveillance
  equipment

Source: eBay Web site.

do my best at the translation. (Letter) "got the photos. what I can see look nice. How many kids you
got?? where do you work out at. just here PW I got a
lot of jealousy in me-I'm not to smart-that's why I
can't get out of the hole. I'm cat K but they won't
even fake that. Charlie Manson" (Note) "Look at it
this-I been lie to + about alot. it's not me xxx-it's you
giving me out for xxx-I already been tricked out of
xxx + it's always turned sour junk. to do it right we
must be true + do it right". Certificate of Authenticity!!! No Reserve!!!³

On the day I checked, eBay listed 122 auctions featuring Charles Manson items. Auctions like these—both
online and off—have stimulated efforts by a number of cit-
izens and public officials to outlaw the sale of items that
might in any way enrich convicted felons. Most states
already have statutes that make it impossible for convicted
felons to make money from the sale of their stories,
through any source. But prior to 2000, no statutes prevented them or anyone else from profiting from the sale of
other items: a lock of hair, a letter, fingernail clippings,
blood samples, and so forth. At the time of this writing,
one California official was introducing legislation to pro-
hibit such sales by auction or other means.
    The company has tried to solve the issue of objec-
tionable items with a blanket policy, as stated on its Web
site:

eBay's community is a diverse, international group of users with varied backgrounds and beliefs, and it's easy to imagine how some items listed on eBay might be offensive to at least some of our users somewhere in the world. But one of eBay's great strengths is the diversity of its membership and the items they trade, and eBay believes that it's important to respect (and learn from) that diversity. That's why eBay generally permits listings of "practically anything on earth," even items which most of us find offensive.

Fundamentally, though, eBay is a community, and members of a community must respect each other as human beings. Listings that promote hate, violence or racial intolerance (or organizations dedicated to such notions) have no place in a true community—we're all here to trade, to do business, and to have fun with each other. eBay will not become a platform for those who promote hatred toward their fellow man. eBay has always exercised judgment in allowing or disallowing certain listings in the best interest of the community. Therefore, eBay will judiciously disallow listings or items that promote hatred, violence, or racial intolerance, including items that promote organizations (such as the KKK, Nazis, neo-Nazis, Skinheads, Aryan Nation) with such views. eBay will review listings that are brought to its attention by the community, and will look at the entire listing to determine whether it falls within this rule. eBay recognizes that some older relics of organizations that promoted hate, violence or racial intolerance are legitimate collectible items that serve as a reminder of past injustices or horrors. Obviously, the past cannot be erased, and such relics can serve as important reminders and educational tools in a community that can learn from the past. Therefore, relics of groups such as the KKK or Nazi Germany may be listed on eBay, provided that they are at least 50 years old, and the listing is not used as a platform to glorify or promote the organization or its values. Listings of such items that are not 50 years old will be removed when brought to our attention. Sellers must state the approximate age of the item within the description.[4]

This statement of policy is probably a consequence of eBay's growing up as a business enterprise. The founding philosophy of letting anyone trade anything with anybody was workable when the company was a small entity, but is not compatible with its current branding efforts or its strategy of forging alliances with Disney, America Online, and other premier companies. The downside of the policy, however, is that it moves the company away from its initial hands-off approach to auction commerce, in which it simply provided a trading venue. That initial approach was amazingly scalable with demand. In laying down a new set of rules, it takes on a policing function, and must act as judge and jury in thousands of gray-area cases. These tasks require time and people, and make the model less scalable.

■ OUTAGES—DOWN BUT NOT OUT

The first major attack of the Internet Age began on Monday, February 7, 2000, when, over the course of several days, cyberpranksters unleashed a rolling assault against the world's biggest e-commerce sites. They went after them one by one, ignoring small targets in favor of the biggest, juiciest targets.

Yahoo! was hit on Monday morning, and was effectively shut down for three hours. Most users who tried to open the portal's home page found themselves locked out. Buy.com was hit the next day, the very day on which the rising young company's shares were going public. You could almost hear its executives and investment bankers moaning "Why us?"

eBay was next on the list. At first, site users found that their pages opened more slowly than normal—say 6 seconds instead of the usual 1.7 or 2. Things deteriorated from that point and stayed that way for several hours. Sellers whose auctions were closing that day were frustrated that few buyers could get in to make their final bids. And the real price action in any online auction usually comes during those last few hours. The site had not been entirely crippled, but its capacity had been cut roughly in half.

CNN and Amazon were hit later that same day. ZDNet, e-Trade, and Datek took their lumps on Wednesday.

And then, as abruptly as they had begun, the attacks ceased. The ambushers slipped away undetected, and commerce on the Internet returned to normal. The only ripples on the surface of the now-calm sea of big-time e-commerce came from company and government officials, who vowed to track down and punish the culprits.

These attacks on the Internet's supertankers were identical in character. Each site's servers were addressed and buried in blizzards of incoming data. Some data took the form of diagnostic messages; others were requests to open site pages. The effect was to crowd out legitimate connections. A company telephone switchboard provides a non-Web analogy. Suddenly, and from many different sources, the switchboard is barraged by incoming calls. Since it can answer only a few calls at a time, most callers fail to get through.

Denial of service (DOS) was the name give to this attack. "Denial of service is like rush-hour on steroids," according to Allan Phillips, a ZDNet executive whose own site came under attack that week. "It's like thousands of people trying to get through the door of the supermarket at the same time." And by all appearances, this one had been launched from dozens of computers owned by unsuspecting individuals and institutions. This proved to be the case. Computers owned by Stanford University, UCLA, and the University of California were among the first of those identified by cybercops in the days that followed. Stanford officials later acknowledged that a university router located at a remote wildlife sanctuary had been hacked and enlisted in the attack on eBay.

eBay's problems with the February caper were actually less severe than they might have been, thanks to the company's long-term plan to scale up its computer infrastructure. During the second half of 1999 it had invested an estimated $30 million in backup servers and other equipment, with the aim of ensuring substantial excess capacity. Whether this investment was part of its more general strategy of scaling up to meet growing demand, or it reflected some forethought about potential DOS attacks, is not clear. Nevertheless, the added capacity dampened the blow.

The February 2000 attack was only the most sensational in a long string of infrastructure problems for eBay—problems that drove its users crazy and that gave

---

THE ANATOMY OF A DOS ATTACK

A hacker uses his or her own PC to break into an innocent third party's network computer. This computer may be the host to dozens if not hundreds of PCs in the network. There the hacker plants a software program that will lurk undetected until the moment of the attack.

At the planned moment, the hacker activates the slave software, which asks each of the networked PCs to respond. But instead of responding to the source, these PCs send their signals to servers of the intended victim. Result: The victim's servers are snowed under with income data, and legitimate users cannot get through.

By design, the slave software leaves no trace of its origin, and the hacker cannot be found.

SYSTEM STATUS

From eBay Announcements, 8 February, 2000

While some users continue to experience slow response times, please understand that this is strictly a "denial of service" attack. This has NOT and does NOT jeopardize data, such as credit card information or auction information.

If your auction is ending tonight and has been materially affected, you can request a credit by writing to billing@ebay.com with the item number(s) of your affected auction(s) and the reason for your credit request.

We continue to take multiple measures to fight this, including working with local and federal authorities, ISPs including Sprint, UUNet and AboveNet, our vendors including Cisco, our partners, and other Internet sites that have recently been attacked in the same way.

We will continue to keep you updated as more information becomes available.

Regards,

eBay[5]

---

company managers nightmares. Server shutdowns plagued the site for several days in late 1998. Even worse was a three-day string of outages in early June 1999. Each of these outages hit the company directly in the cash box.

Following the DOS attack, Meg Whitman tried to put the best possible face on that latest event when she told newsmen that "if a user comes on and the site isn't functioning perfectly, they'll often come back three or four hours later and list their item [for sale] or make a bid. . . . It's not like an airplane seat where after the airplane leaves that seat has gone wasted." The amount of $80,000 was cited, primarily for engineering overtime payments.[6]

This estimate seems highly optimistic. First, eBay has a practice of refunding listing fees. A one-day outage in June 1999 cost the company an estimated $3 to $5 million in refunds to sellers.[7] Cahners In-Stat Group has in fact estimated the cost of a single-day outage at $2.8 million for an auction site, and almost twice that amount for an online brokerage.[8] The real costs of site outages for eBay may be less quantifiable but equally large. Both sellers and bidders are frustrated and turned off when an outage throws a monkey wrench into their auctions, and some of these will either migrate to other auction sites or give up on the auction game entirely, diminishing future revenues. Further, the angst generated by outages tarnishes the positive brand image that eBay works so hard and spends so liberally to create. And as for lost revenues, there is neither evidence nor logic to support Whitman's contention that fees lost during outages are recouped. That doesn't happen in retail sales, and there is no reason to believe that it happens in auction markets.

■ GROWING PAINS WILL GO AWAY

Schemers, scammers, hackers, counterfeiters, crashers, and complainers: In the Wild West days of the Internet, these are part of the landscape. Why should we expect anything else?

Like every new market, the online auction phenomenon needs time to work out the kinks, reach agreements on standards, achieve system stability, clean out the bums, and achieve system stability. Each of these improvements will happen as eBay and competing sites grow up and become more mature. During this period we are likely to see greater collaboration between the company and the trade groups who represent copyright holders. This is already happening. Expect, too, to see an evolving consensus about what is and what is *not* an acceptable auction item. Like the telephone company, eBay is poorly equipped to police the traffic that crosses its wires. But it will have to take a larger responsibility for what gets auctioned on its site and for the few but troublesome creeps who prey on members of the eBay nation.

Outages, too, are bound to become fewer and shorter. Early phone systems had plenty of outages. Today, they are rare.

Hackers are another story. It's hard to see a future without them. Somewhere in the distribution curve of human genetics there is a chromosome that instructs males under the age of 25 to attack or undermine the smug, the complacent, and other lumbering targets of opportunity. This same "H" chromosome inspires MIT undergraduates to put campus police cars on top of the school's landmark dome during the dead of the night, and compels students everywhere to short-sheet their room-mates' beds. It may even have been responsible for the Sack of Rome and the Hundred Years' War. If you think the cybercops can make the world safe from these characters, forget it. It's in the gene pool.

The same with scammers. As long as money is to be had, there will be goofballs aplenty trying to find a short-cut to it.

The only question is what they'll try next.

Chapter

8

Competing for
the Future

■ AMAZON'S CORPORATE STRATEGY ■ OTHER ENTRANTS
■ THE ECLIPSE OF P2P AUCTIONS? ■ THE AUCTION
AGGREGATORS ■ THOUSANDS OF WINNERS
■ LESSONS FROM EBAY

The market for person-to-person Internet trading in early 1999 was relatively young, changing fast, and a matter of intense and growing competition. Auction sites were sprouting like spring daffodils. "It was nerve-wracking," confessed Benchmark's Bob Kagle, "when we saw one competitive assault after another being mounted."

It started with Onsale, which was already established as a popular business-to-consumer site. Onsale had tremendous resources and made a substantial marketing effort in launching its person-to-person auction site. Yahoo!, Lycos, Excite, Microsoft's MSN, and many small niche sites followed—no doubt spurred on by eBay's obvious success and the low cost of entry. Looking for something special to lure sellers their way, some eliminated the usual seller charges.

All found the going tough. Yahoo!Auctions came onstream in the summer of 1999 with an impressive array of buyer and seller services but failed to make much of a dent. As described by AuctionWatch.com, "To understand what ails Yahoo!Auctions, all you have to do is visit its message boards. It's quiet—real quiet—underscoring one of the site's real dilemmas: lack of community and user loyalty."

"It's been difficult for us to build up our site [to close] to a million listings," a Yahoo! spokesman conceded to AuctionWatch.com. "It's taken us a year to do so, and we started when eBay was only listing 700,000 items."[1] Later entrants would have even greater difficulty in gaining traction.

The 1,000-pound gorilla of the Internet stepped into the person-to-person auction market in April 1999. With close to 8 million customers, 16 million available products, and site features that benefited from eBay's experimentation and mistakes, Amazon.com's entry to online auctions came on like a strong right hook, knocking eBay's share price down by $15 in a single day. eBay was big medicine in e-commerce, but Amazon was far bigger. Some 101 million U.S. adults recognized the Amazon name, but only 63 million recognized eBay.

The Internet fraternity watched the Amazon-eBay matchup with interest and anticipation. Amazon was always entering new areas—it aimed to cover the known universe. But this was the first time it had butted heads with an established online rival, and its progress—or lack of progress—would say much about its ability to hold its own in a future, more mature Internet marketplace.

Amazon's new auction site was remarkably similar to eBay's. There was no question as to the origin of its format and features. User agreements and logistics were strikingly similar. By design, any eBay user would feel right at home at Amazon and have no problem negotiating the site. There were also important pluses. Sellers got a no-fee deal for several months as the site scaled up. They could also obtain free cross-promotion to relevant Amazon retail sites. For example, a seller auctioning an autographed picture of Bruce Springsteen might be able to link the auction to an Amazon site retailing the Boss's latest CD.

Amazon also upped the ante on buyer guarantees. Its A-to-Z Guarantee aimed to underwrite the risks of (1) a seller failing to send an item that was bought and paid for, and (2) a purchased item being "materially different" from the seller's description.

Many were impressed by some of the newcomer's features. According to AuctionWatch.com, a service that monitors and evaluates auction sites, Amazon "has outclassed the competition in the area of customer service"[2]—a chronically problematic area for eBay. "Long-term customer service for new users is eBay's biggest cross to bear," AuctionWatch continued in its review. "Currently, new users are falling through the cracks. The site is simply unable to keep pace with the number of customer service queries it receives." Amazon claimed greater strength in this important area.

With its online auction now launched, Amazon's earlier investment of $45 million for a small stake in Sotheby's brick-and-mortar auction house made perfect sense. Sotheby's gave Amazon a strategic anchor in the high end of the market, where fee revenues were bound to be high. And as time went by, the site improved its customer convenience; it added features like Amazon.com Payment, which facilitated the use of credit-card purchases, while eBay users were still struggling with sending personal checks and money orders.

The new auction site got off to a good start, reaching about 100,000 auctions per day by late summer 1999. But then the number of listings stalled out, particularly after the free ride for sellers was over.

If sellers were not joining the party as anticipated, buyers weren't either. Even in the books category, symbolically Amazon's strongest suit, traffic was thin. AuctionWatch cited an anemic 45 bids on a total of 883 book auctions held at about that time.[3] Many auctions were expiring without a single bid—a huge disappointment for sellers.

As a late-to-the-party player, Amazon had run into the teeth of the auction market's iron rule: buyers and sellers go where the action is hottest—that is, where the *liquidity* is greatest. Keenan Vision noted in an earlier report that "eBay has found a natural feedback loop where creating a critical mass of bidders increases the price obtained by sellers, which increases the number of sellers, which attracts more bidders, et cetera."[4] Breaking into that loop is extremely difficult. It's like getting job experience: If you don't already have it, no employer wants to give it to you. Larry (aka wishmaker) summed up the view of many veteran eBay sellers: "I've posted auctions on just about every site you can imagine [but] I pretty much stick with eBay." His reason for channeling most of his business through eBay is straightforward and representative of those Amazon hoped to attract. "The buyers are there [on eBay]. I'm established there. My feedback rating establishes me as an upstanding member of the community. I don't have those ratings on other sites because I don't do much business on any of them. I'd rather stay where I'm known."

Another eBay regular offered this chat room advice: "I love the format at Yahoo! and at Amazon. But ya gotta be where it's at."

But Amazon wasn't finished giving its rival headaches. On September 30, 1999, it opened zShops, a move that aimed to create an Internet shopping bazaar in which merchants large and small could retail their goods. On Day 1, zShops offered half a million items, roughly four times the number of items carried by the average Kmart store: artwork, antiques, books, cars, coins and stamps, computer hardware and software, music, movies, toys—the whole nine yards. "We will be a place to find anything," CEO Jeff Bezos told the press.

Amazon's goal was to become the world's biggest shopping mall. Success would elevate its drawing power on the net relative to America Online, Yahoo!, and other higher-traffic portals. zShops also aimed to attract the thousands of small merchants who were anxious to use the Web as a new distribution channel—including those currently selling through eBay. zShops was a quick and easy way to do it.

zShops promised to be good medicine for Amazon, which by that point in time had managed to lose nearly half a billion dollars. A stream of cash from monthly fees charged to listing merchants and a 4.75 percent charge against all sales for which Amazon processed credit-card purchases would keep revenues growing and help support the company's enormous stock price. And unlike Amazon's book and CD sales businesses, zShops would require no inventory, warehouses, or other fixed assets on the part of the Net giant. All responsibilities for inventory, billing, and shipping would belong to participating z-merchants. It was very similar to eBay's hands-off, fee-based business model. All Amazon had to do was run the site and collect its fees.

zShops was very attractive to many small merchants in that it gave them access to Amazon's growing legions of customers, which then numbered 11 million. Larger merchandisers were less thrilled, because Amazon would stand between them and the customers with whom they aimed to build long-term relationships.

■ AMAZON'S CORPORATE STRATEGY

Jeff Bezos and his team lead the Internet in creating red ink. However, they are strategically prepared to sacrifice profits in the short term to build their business and capture markets. The company's heady stock price abets this strategy, providing high-priced stock to fund expansion and purchase hard assets. Investors appear willing to play along as long as there is a reasonable expectation of someday producing operating income commensurate with the company's high market value.

As CFO Joy Covey explained to *Forbes* in 1999, if Amazon can generate $10 billion in revenues per year, with a gross margin of 20 percent (like Wal-Mart), and keep its operating expenses down to $1 billion, it will produce $1

billion in operating income (i.e., income before depreciation, interest, and taxes). This, in her opinion, will produce a return on invested capital sufficient to justify the
company's market cap.[5]

The big gorilla's entry into the auction market
couldn't have come at a worse time for eBay. Rapid growth
was complicating eBay's ability to provide adequate customer service. A few highly visible scams had taken place.
And there had been a streak of service outages. These
shortcomings were upsetting to the volume sellers on
whom Omidyar and company depended. To many of these
sellers, the grass might appear greener over on the new,
fresh Amazon site. Would they walk?

In an interview with *Upside*'s Chuck Lenatti, eBay's
Meg Whitman indicated that her company had anticipated Amazon's entry into the auction market for some
time, and professed to take it seriously. "Amazon executes
incredibly well," she said, "and it's a very serious competitor to eBay."

> [But] we created this market and we know it really
> well. We have a bit of a "network effect" business
> here: The more buyers you have, the more sellers
> you have, [and] in turn, [that] attracts more buyers.
> As a result, it's difficult to get competitive lift-off
> versus eBay because we've achieved such scale in a
> small amount of time. We also have some advan-
> tages in customer support. The person-to-person
> marketplace requires a lot of customer support,
> because you are dealing largely with individuals
> [who] have varying degrees of technical knowl-
> edge.[6]

After noting that Amazon was in a number of other
businesses, she told *Upside* readers that:

> This is the only business we're in, and it's a full-
> time, 24-by-7 job to make person-to-person trading

on the Internet fun, fast, entertaining and easy to use. [Also], our market is very mass market. Our users are old and young, employed and unemployed, male and female, [representing] a very wide spectrum of the American demographic. I suspect because [Amazon's audience] is largely book purchasers, and a small percentage of Americans actually purchase books, [that] they're probably pretty well-educated individuals. It's quite a different customer base than ours.[7]

Whitman also emphasized the issues important to eBay sellers, the users who account for all of its revenues.

What is most important to sellers is [whether] their item sells and [whether] they feel like they got the best price for that item. [They measure] how many bids they got and [whether there was] some action on their item. A very high percentage of our auctions close—far higher than any competitor's—and there's more action on any individual sale. It comes back to the network effects of this business. I anticipate that some of our buyers and sellers will try Amazon, and I expect they'll come back.[8]

Whitman clearly gave her company's customer service higher marks than did either regular user or site reviewers at the time. Still, her assessment of buyers and sellers sticking with eBay has proven correct.

■ OTHER ENTRANTS

Amazon wasn't the only threat to eBay's early dominance of the person-to-person auction market. Barriers to entry being relatively low, some 800 auction sites popped up between 1995 and 2000, many inspired by eBay's success. Most were highly specialized. With eBay being inundated with listers, these sites appealed to sellers' fears of being lost in the crowd. Almost all, however, suffered from the same lack of critical mass that undercut the commercial potential of Yahoo! and Amazon auctions. Buyers and sellers wanted to be where the action was greatest.

Another serious threat to eBay appeared at a most auspicious time—a day in mid-September 1999, on which its system was down (again). This time it wasn't a single challenger but an alliance of powerful Internet players. Several major e-commerce sites announced that they would form an auction *network*. The network would include Microsoft's MSN, Excite@Home, Lycos, and Fair-Market, the network's lynchpin. eBay stock tumbled $10 on the news.

The FairMarket network is a business-to-consumer auction network connecting leading portal sites, online communities, and vendors on the Web. When it went online in September 1999, it boasted a combined reach of 46 million users, eight times larger than eBay's user base at the time. Each community site connected to a single database of merchandise. For example, computer liquidations listed by Dell at www.dellauction.com automatically appeared on all networked auction sites, including those hosted by Microsoft, Excite, and Lycos.

Alta Vista soon joined the network, as did Xoom.com, Outpost.com, ZDNet, CompUSA, and Ticketmaster. As members of the FairMarket network, shoppers on these sites had access to goods and services from many sites without having to go to other URLs. Keeping people in place was the whole point for MSN and other portal sites.

FairMarket aimed to appeal to the big merchandisers who didn't want their brand-name products to share listing space with the collectibles and assorted used junk sold by amateurs.

Appealing as this concept may seem, a site tour made six months after its start-up indicated that eBay probably had little to fear from this coalition of competing auction sites. Many product categories were sparsely populated, listing only two or three items. Those that did contain many listings offered little product variety. For example, being in the market for one of the new writable CD drives, I looked under CD-RW but found only *one* machine listed. There were 20 other listings under CD-RW, but each listing was for an identical item: a package of blank writable CDs—commodity products that anyone could find anywhere, and all listed by the same seller. So where was the variety? Where was the sizzle? Like other categories, most of these items I viewed had received no bids by the time I checked in, even though they had been posted several days earlier.

From what I could see, the FairMarket auction network simply isn't fun. Nothing about the site raised my anticipation of finding something unique, or of encountering an interesting seller. There was no community, no eclectism. It was all standard products straight out of manufacturers' shipping cartons. But FairMarket is still a newcomer. It might gain traction with time.

■ THE ECLIPSE OF P2P AUCTIONS?

The invasion of name-brand merchandisers on FairMarket, Amazon, Online, and other sites is bound to upset the balance of market power currently enjoyed by eBay, even though their current impacts have been less than spectacular. Over the long haul, business-to-consumer (B2C) auctions seem destined to shoulder out person-to-person (P2P) auctions in terms of transaction numbers, participants, and gross sales. The reason is simple: for manufacturers, retailers, and airlines alike, auctions are an efficient way to liquidate unwanted inventory. Instead of dumping stock onto liquidators for pennies on the dollar, they can capture far higher values through auctions.

Forecasts developed by Forrester Research project B2C auctions growing to $12.6 billion by the end of 2003, roughly doubling the total of P2P auctions, led by computer hardware, travel, autos, and general apparel (Figure 8.1). Forrester believes that the great mass of consumers will prefer buying from established, name-brand companies rather than from individuals, and it is probably correct. This is how most merchandise is bought.

Even if Forrester's hypothesis is correct, there is plenty of room for both types of auctions in cyberspace. And nothing in eBay's business model precludes it from branching into B2C auctions. Indeed, in an interview with *BusinessWeek,* Meg Whitman opened the door to this form of commerce:

> We are looking at storefronts as something to think about. Now, all the selling on eBay is an auction format. And the question is: Are there other formats both our buyers and sellers would want? There are people who don't necessarily like to buy in an auction, and there are sellers who want to sell some of their goods in an auction and some in a storefront,

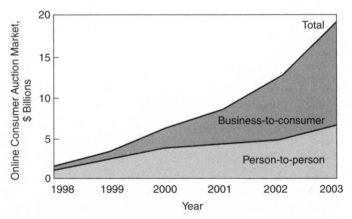

Figure 8.1 Forecasted business-to-consumer and person-to-person auctions, through 2003. (*From Forrester Research. Used with permission.*)

sort of a fixed-price environment. So we are looking at this."[9]

Will eBay, like rival Amazon, splinter into different
formats on the same site? Whitman's statement suggests a
better than even chance. If it happens, however, it will be
rolled out carefully and with substantial preparation. "I
have this philosophy," she told the same publication, "that
you really need to do things 100 percent. Better to do five
things at 100 percent than 10 things at 80 percent."[10]

■ THE AUCTION AGGREGATORS

The newest challenge to eBay's position arose in the fall of
1999 with the appearance of *auction aggregators* such as
AuctionWatch.com, Auction Rover, and Bidder's Edge.
These sites collect listings directly from eBay and other
auctions and then aggregate them on their own sites.
Aggregated data makes it possible for bidders to compare
prices and monitor many auctions at once. So, if a buyer is
looking for a classical guitar, he or she can conduct a
search from a single site, not the five or six where this type
of item is normally found. As Bidder's Edge tells its visitors, "The tools and services offered by Bidder's Edge, Inc.
help on-line auction users easily and automatically find
great bargains from many on-line auctions all from a single 'portal-like' Web site."

eBay viewed these aggregators as infringers and threatened legal action, claiming that they were unlawfully
accessing its site, making unauthorized copies of its content, and displaying that content in incomplete and con-
fusing ways. But this threat did little to stop the aggregators.
Attempts by eBay to control their activities through licensing agreements also failed, with the exception of Auction
Rover and another small company. Those proposed agreements included both a fee and a requirement that eBay

results not be listed with those of other auctions sites. "If you want to do comparative shopping," AuctionWatch marketing executive Dan Neary stated in our interview, "you need to have results side-by-side." AuctionWatch wouldn't play ball.

The danger posed by the auction aggregators was clear: eBay's greatest competitive strength was its transaction volume. Sellers flocked to it because it had the most sellers and the most buyers. If buyers could monitor auctions from another site, then sellers theoretically had less incentive to list on eBay. Buyers would see their merchandise whether they listed on Yahoo!, Amazon, or any one of the niche sites. And some of these other sites charged less and had reputations for better seller support. Aggregator sites also posed a threat to the sense of community that eBay had worked so hard to foster.

eBay's threat of legal action was enough to make Bidder's Edge initially back off. "We're a $9 million company [and] they're a multibillion dollar company," a Bidder's Edge executive told the press. "We think we would ultimately win a court battle, but . . . we don't have the resources to fight them."[11] AuctionWatch was less easily intimidated. Its universal search technology gave it the capability to mine data from over 300 different sites and aggregate them in convenient formats. "We've launched the service because the auction community was asking for it," the company's cofounder Rodrigo Sales told *Forbes* in an October 1999 interview. "Buyers want a wider selection, and sellers want more exposure for their auctions so they can get the highest price."[12] In his view, eBay's content was in the public domain. eBay acknowledged that it did not own the descriptions and the photos submitted by sellers. However, it claimed that other key information (e.g., the number of bids, the length of the auction, etc.) were produced by eBay and were, therefore, its property.

Even as the war of words raged, eBay enlisted technical countermeasures to block AuctionWatch's ability to gather auction data from its site. That worked for over a month, until AuctionWatch devised software capable of getting through.

Both Bidder's Edge and AuctionWatch were successful in aggregating data from eBay and other leading sites. eBay continued to resist, though with little success. In April 2000, however, eBay won a nonbinding decision from a federal judge, barring Bidder's Edge from further crawling the eBay site. Final resolution of this and similar cases will no doubt bring some clarity to a fundamental issue of the Internet Age—namely, what information is public and what is private and proprietary?

As insurance against any judicial finding unfavorable to its interests, eBay went to Washington as a backer of the Collections of Information Antipiracy Act. Known as the Coble bill, because of its House of Representatives sponsor Howard Coble, a North Carolina Republican, this piece of legislation aimed to protect the creators of databases against the data-gathering and -using activities of aggregators and many other e-commerce companies while ensuring fair-use exceptions for researchers and educators. In the view of Coble, eBay, and other supporters of the bill, this protection was needed to secure the incentives of database creators. The Coble bill had powerful opponents, including Yahoo!, Amazon, leading universities, the American Library Association, AT&T, and Reuters, to name a few. In their view, the Coble bill would give database creators monopoly control over value-added downstream uses of information. These forces rallied around the Consumer and Investor Access to Information Act sponsored by Virginia Republican Tom Bliley.

Ironically, eBay's threats and legal defenses against the aggregators have indirectly triggered a U.S. Department of Justice probe of its operations. That investigation aims to determine if eBay's practices are stifling competition. If the Justice Department's findings go against it, and if sanctions follow, the company's attempts to shut out the data aggregators will be seen as a major mistake.

AUCTION SITE COMPARISON

AuctionWatch.com of San Bruno, California, provides periodic reviews of individual auction sites and a summary comparison. Here is the comparison it provided in April 2000.

AW Auction Ratings
See how AuctionWatch sizes up your favorite auction site, based on six important criteria: Inventory, Bidding Activity, Services and Fees, Customer Support, Design and Functionality, and Community.

Auction Site	Inventory	Bidding Activity	Services & Fees	Customer Support	Design & Functionality	Community
321 Gone	○	○	○	●	●	○
Alta Vista Auctions	●	○	○	●	○	○
Amazon.com Auctions	●	○	●	●	●	○
AuctionAddict.com	○	○	●	●	○	○
Auctions.com	●	○	●	●	●	○
boxLot	○	○	●	●	○	○
CityAuction	○	○	●	●	●	○
CNET Auctions	●	○	○	○	●	○
Collecting Nation	○	○	●	●	○	●
ComicExchange.Net	●	○	●	○	●	○
eBay	●	●	●	○	●	●
edeal	○	○	●	●	○	●
eHammer	●	●	●	●	○	○
eRock.net	○	○	○	○	●	●
eWanted.com	○	○	●	●	●	○
Excite Auctions	○	○	●	●	○	○
First Auction	○	●	○	●	●	N/A
GoAuction	●	○	●	●	●	○
Gold's Auction	○	○	●	●	●	●
Go Network Auction	○	○	●	●	●	○
Haggle Online	○	○	●	○	○	○
Lycos Auctions	○	○	●	●	●	○
MSN Auctions	●	○	●	○	●	○
Musichotbid.com	●	○	○	●	○	○
NiceBid	○	○	●	●	○	○
Onsale	●	●	○	●	○	N/A
Popula	○	●	●	●	○	●
SportsAuction	●	N/A	○	●	●	N/A
Teletrade	○	N/A	●	●	○	N/A
uBid	○	●	●	○	●	N/A
Up4Sale	●	○	○	○	●	○
Yahoo Auctions	●	●	●	○	●	○

● = Excellent ● = Good ○ = Average ○ = Below Average

Source: AuctionWatch, www.auctionwatch.com/awdaily/reviews/ratings.html.

■ THOUSANDS OF WINNERS

Members of the business press, like their brethren in sports journalism, love to frame wide-ranging and complex competitive issues in terms of a duel between just a few companies. "eBay vs. Amazon" *BusinessWeek* proclaimed in a 1999 cover story. Under such headings as "Battle Royal," and "The Duel Extends to Wall Street," the media has represented the evolution of online shopping as a rough-and-tumble contest from which one winner will emerge. If you buy into this approach you can almost picture Jeff Bezos and Meg Whitman duking it out, with the loser retreating into commercial obscurity. However, consumer e-commerce is not a zero-sum game. So many millions will be flocking to the Internet and online shopping in the foreseeable future that Amazon, eBay, and many other sites—large and small—will be winners. Some will garner more daily hits than others. Some will boast higher revenues than others. Some will have lower revenues but higher absolute profits.

Nor will online shoppers look to one site to meet all of their needs. Consumers don't spend all of the time at one brick-and-mortar store, so why should we believe their online behavior will be any different? In the world of traditional merchandising, as in cyberspace, being the biggest doesn't keep people from moving their purchasing choices around. General Motors is the largest auto maker, but that fact hasn't kept millions of consumers from buying from Ford, DaimlerChrysler, Toyota, Volvo, and other manufacturers. Wal-Mart is a giant among U.S. retail merchandisers, but the people who go there to buy sneakers for their kids generally go elsewhere to buy their books, office supplies, and laptop computers.

Consumers schlep around from one pile of bricks and mortar to another all the time, even though it involves lots of driving, parking, walking through snowdrifts, and other annoyances. Because moving from site to site on the Internet is infinitely easier and less time consuming, why would anyone expect shoppers to go to one Internet site and stay there?

If I need to buy several newly published books on e-commerce, I click onto Amazon, where I can see at a glance the most current titles on that subject. If I'm lucky, other Amazon users will have provided reviews of these works—something that really adds value for me. If I were shopping for a personal computer and printer for a kid heading off to college, I'd head for a site that features lots of model close-outs, factory-refurbished gear, and inventory liquidations. A kid doesn't need state-of-the art equipment to surf the Net and write Composition 101 papers. If garden supplies are what I need, I won't go to any of the major sites. I'll log onto Garden.com, where a black-thumbed guy like me can get lots of expert advice about what to plant where and when. This site will have all the hard-to-find specialty items I might need: a garden planning template, bulbs, seeds, books, and tools. It will even tell me how to make my garden more attractive to songbirds. That's what I call value-added merchandising.

When I'm on the prowl for a unique item—an older musical instrument or a rare book—eBay will be my first stop. This is the kind of merchandise that antique and specialty shops have always provided. The site is fun, funky, and always provides surprises. You'll never find these items or this funky ambiance at Wal-Mart or Best Buy, and you're not likely to find them at the online sites that feature the same name-brand products.

So we shouldn't waste our time trying to identify who will be king of the Internet. There will be many crowned heads.

In the final analysis, what constitutes "winning" in online merchandising means different things to different people. Investors, of course, define winners as those dot-coms that generate the greatest dividends and capital appreciation over time. (You may be doubling over with laughter at my using the terms *dividends* and *dot-coms* in the same sentence. However, the value of an ongoing business's stock is ultimately determined by its ability to share profits through a stream of dividends—payable either now or in the future.)

The different seller groups have their own definitions of *winning:*

- *Business-to-consumer sellers.* A winning site for these sellers is one where they can quickly and efficiently move merchandise, both first-run and closeout, while protecting their brand images.

- *Small-dealer-to-consumer sellers.* These sellers will stick with sites that give them geographic reach—including local markets for automobiles and other hard-to-ship items—and millions of potential buyers. To date, eBay has been the ideal site for these sellers and is challenged only by the emergence of zShops, a fixed-price site.

- *Person-to-person sellers.* Sites that provide buyer depth, good prices, ease of use, and antifraud protections will be winners in the eyes of these sellers. Here again, eBay is the name to beat. As CEO Meg Whitman told *Upside:*

What is most important to sellers is [whether] their item sells and [whether] they feel like they got the best price for that item. [They measure] how many bids they got and [whether there was] some action on their item. A very high percentage of our auctions close—far higher than any competitor's—and there's more action on any individual sale. It comes back to the network effects of this business. I anticipate that some of our buyers and sellers will try Amazon, and I expect they'll come back.[13]

■ LESSONS FROM EBAY

As of spring 2000, eBay remains unchallenged as the king of the person-to-person auction market, with a market share of over 90 percent. The challengers are out there, and working hard to unseat the leader. In AuctionWatch's assessment:

> It has overcome the biggest obstacle facing every online auction site: establishing a massive community of buyers and sellers. This in itself minimizes the chances of being burned—every auction users' greatest fear. eBay will stand uncontested until the other major auction sites can level the playing field. If and when that happens, eBay's design and customer service issues will certainly surface as the site's Achilles' heel. That's where eBay is the most vulnerable and the competition can make significant inroads.[14]

eBay's success in its chosen market niche suggests a number of important lessons for any firm that aims for success in person-to-person online commerce:

- *For auction sites: Control the lion's share of transactions.* Buyers and sellers gravitate to the site with the greatest volume of participants—the network effect.
- *Provide a large and interesting selection of goods.* Product depth and variety attract buyers, which in turn will attract more sellers.
- *Achieve system reliability.* Outages are costly and undermine user loyalty.
- *Provide high-quality customer service.* Users need to have their questions answered and their problems resolved, otherwise they will stop trading or go elsewhere.

- *Assure the reliability of user deliveries and payments.* These are absolute requirements for site credibility.

- *Enhance brand recognition.* With millions of net users coming onstream in the years ahead, brand recognition is the surest single mechanism for increasing new site users and increasing transaction volume.

- *Increase Web site convenience and accessibility.* If a site is easy to access and navigate, more people will log on, stay longer, and make more transactions.

- *Develop high-quality search tools.* People will not buy what they cannot locate quickly on the site.

Chapter

9

Whither eBay

■ EXTENDING THE PLATFORM ■ TOWARD A BETTER
END-TO-END SOLUTION ■ THE GLOBAL CHALLENGE
■ FUTURE SCENARIOS

As late as the spring of 2000, things were looking rosy for eBay. Usership was growing and all knowledgeable analysts were predicting that that growth would continue. The company's proactive approach to outage prevention appeared to be working. Initiatives aimed at solidifying relationships with volume sellers and keeping them in the fold were paying off. eBay's people were still thinking that they hadn't yet seen the potential limits to their business expansion. The company had become a household word and a regular source of shopping and entertainment for millions of people—something that few businesses anywhere or at any time in the past could claim in so short a time. In their view, the upside potential remained unbounded.

So, what does the future hold?

With its share price in the $76 range (following its 2-for-1 split), eBay has the financial wherewithal to acquire other, unrelated business—real businesses with real honest-to-goodness earnings. Other Internet companies with inflated market capitalizations have followed this route. And why not? That is exactly what big traditional companies with lots of cash and equity value have done for years. When their own growth curves begin to flatten, they use their financial muscle to acquire younger, more dynamic businesses in a bid to rejuvenate their flagging fortunes. Not so eBay. Its executives see nothing but blue sky ahead. They continue to execute within their original business plan, acquiring only those companies that can assist in that execution. Analysts and other eBay watchers, however, perceive four major challenges:

- Building systems capacity and systems reliability apace with growth
- Extending the eBay platform to new goods categories
- Creating a more complete customer solution
- Going global

The first of these challenges is, in large part, already overcome. Working with its suppliers, eBay has spent royally on building substantial excess system capacity and greater reliability. The other challenges, however, will test the company in the years ahead.

■ EXTENDING THE PLATFORM

The "bear case" against eBay, as Donaldson, Lufkin & Jenrette's (DLJ's) Jamie Kiggen describes it, is that the market for the company's brand of auctions is limited to the types of goods normally sold through flea markets, garage sales, public auctions, and classified ads. Kiggen doesn't buy this view. But even if this were true, plenty of unconquered terrain remains in key segments of the person-to-person market, particularly in high-value goods categories such as automobiles, furniture, appliances, and boats. The addition of the Business Exchange has doubled or tripled the potential of those currently unexploited areas. Creating a greater presence in these higher-end segments and solving associated logistical problems will surely occupy eBay staff for years to come. The rewards for success, however, will be substantial, as exploitation of these categories could easily double the final value of the *average* auction from its current $47. The financial mathematics is compelling: more auctions at higher values translate into both higher gross revenues and disproportionately larger operating profit.

And who knows what other categories of goods (or services) may be opened in the future? The auction platform is amazingly robust. Almost anything can be traded on it.

Success in platform extension is likely but not assured. Many potential customers will prefer fixed-price exchanges over the auction format, and local and regional newspapers are likely to fight back with auction sites of their own.

■ TOWARD A BETTER END-TO-END SOLUTION

Every well-managed enterprise periodically takes an outside-in look at itself, asking: "How difficult is it for our customers to do business with us?" These companies know that anything that creates difficulty for customers reduces the number of transactions and gross revenues. For example, in the early 1990s, independent researchers hired by Polaroid Corporation asked some 3,000 photographic dealers and distributors how they liked doing business with Polaroid. These customers gave the company a low rating relative to its best-in-class competitors, pointing to problems with returns, order entry, billing errors, slow credit approvals, poor delivery reliability, and frustration in reaching the right person through customer service. "You have to talk to 25 people to get an answer," one dealer complained.[1] Each of these problems represented a barrier that customers had to overcome just to do business with the film and imaging company. Once the extent of the problem was understood, the company initiated a far-reaching reengineering of its customer fulfillment functions with the goal of making doing business with Polaroid "as easy as taking an instant picture." Before long, daily measurements of customer service response times and execution quality showed dramatic improvement. Doing business with Polaroid had become easier.

Like Polaroid before it made major changes, eBay has much unfinished business with respect to the *end-to-end experience* of its users. Its auction process contains many barriers, particularly for sellers. There is a substantial learning process involved in creating JPEG files, uploading them to the Web, and linking each with particular auction listings. And once an auction closes with a winning bid, the seller must e-mail the high bidder, saying "You won the auction; here's where to send the check or money order." Then there is the packing and shipping, both laborious processes. Particularly for inexperienced sellers, these represent frictions in the transaction cycle that throw cold water on business growth.

The use of personal checks and money orders for auction payments has been one of the biggest barriers to transaction efficiency. As of March 2000, over 90 percent of transactions on eBay were still being settled by these forms of payment. Personal check payment means that purchased items are not being shipped until the winning bidder's check arrives through the mail and is cleared by the buyer's bank. That might be an 8- to 12-day cycle. This is at a time when people can order a uniquely configured PC from Dell or Gateway and expect delivery at their doorsteps in 4 to 5 business days! People expect more—and they are getting it in other consumer markets. As Bob Kagle mused in our interview, "I think that eBay needs to do a better job of end-to-end trading solutions."[2]

In point of fact, a long effort of continuous, incremental improvements by the company has aimed at creating those solutions. Services such as iEscrow, e-Stamp, Mister Lister, and iShip were all steps in this direction. In late

1999 the company released a beta version of the Billpoint credit-card payment system to 5,000 registered users. This system makes it possible for a buyer to use his or her credit card even if the seller does not have a merchant credit-card account, which for nondealer sellers is generally the case. The expectation is that check settlements will become a thing of the past within a year or so of Billpoint's complete rollout.

Collectively, these services have progressively simplified auction transactions for buyers and sellers. They may fall short of a complete and seamless solution, but many incremental improvements over time often achieve a similar result. The My eBay feature is one good example. My eBay is a feature that allows users to keep track of all their bidding and selling activities, their recent rating feedback, and their current account status with eBay. Over a period of six months or so, beginning in late 1999, a number of small and often unnoticed changes to this feature gave it new functionality and an improved look and feel. eBay will be under pressure to continue improvements like this for all key aspects of its user interface in the years ahead.

■ THE GLOBAL CHALLENGE

eBay's greatest opportunity for future growth lies beyond its North American market. "Management has been very good at identifying high return-on-investment opportunities," according to DLJ's Jamie Kiggen, "[and] international will be a massive opportunity for them." Amazon has also recognized the opportunity and will provide stiff competition. Commenting in an AuctionWatch article, Jeff Blackburn, general manager of Amazon.com Auctions, anticipated global auctioning as one of the primary trends for his industry, and one that "only the most technologically advanced and heavily resourced sites will be able to achieve."[3]

The company has already established beachheads in Great Britain, Australia, Germany, and Japan, and others will surely follow. These nationcentric trading communities represent opportunities both for revenue expansion and for learning how to deal with unique cultural and business practices. Going hand-in-hand with those opportunities are very real risks that the company will become bogged down in mastering the nuances of these markets, and that revenue growth will remain profitless for a number of years.

The much knottier problem will be generating cross-border trade—that is, bringing everyone under a *single* eBay tent. The idea of cross-border auctions is, nevertheless, immensely appealing. Imagine, for instance, the fun that Europeans will have looking over and bidding on the diaries of American Civil War soldiers, or that Americans will have in bidding on letters and documents signed by notables of English arts and letters. Cross-border auctions will open new realms of collecting and entertaining exploration.

The Internet currently delivers the eBay home page to every city and town on the face of the globe, but complications with different languages and currencies, customs regulations and inspections, and trade rules produce substantial barriers to efficient trading. A transaction between a seller in India and a buyer in Indiana, for example, creates substantial difficulties that must be solved before the benefits of a single trading community can be enjoyed by the company and its users.

■ FUTURE SCENARIOS

eBay has come a long way in its short life, and analysts who follow the company predict continued rapid growth in all key metric (users, gross revenues, and gross merchandise sales) in 2001 and 2002. Even more striking, it has catalyzed the formation of many other enterprises: auction aggregators, providers of software tools and seller services (e.g., iEscrow and iShip), and thousands of small-dealer businesses. Still other enterprises, from Barr's Fiddle Shop to the U.S. Postal Service, have expanded their existing operations thanks to eBay. By some estimates, 5 percent of all packages currently delivered by the U.S. Postal Service contain items won by eBay bidders. In this sense, the little operation that began in Pierre Omidyar's living room in 1995 has created a tremendous ripple effect in the economy.

Collectively, eBay and the many enterprises that operate in its shadow are generating substantial economic activity. Some of that activity has come off the plates of local flea markets, used-car dealers, and the classified ads of local newspapers. But most of it represents all *new* economic activity.

The big question for eBay watchers today is: What will this company look like in five years? Most analysts are betting that it will keep on growing at its current rate for two or three more years, and then experience the usual tapering off that comes with market maturation. But because no one, not even its founders and earlier supporters, had any idea that their little company would grow and develop in the way it has, its probably wiser to think in terms of a *range* of possible outcomes instead of a particular forecast. After all, the Internet economy is constantly surprising those who are closest to it. The only thing we can say with certainty is that eBay will change.

Here are some scenarios that come to mind (all attributed statements are fabricated):

- *eBay acquired.* Yahoo! buys eBay and pulls the plug on its own struggling auction site. Yahoo! management wisely gives its subsidiary far-reaching operational automony, and uses its own home page as the port of entry to eBay auctions.

- *eBay on an acquisition bender.* eBay uses its own shares and long-term debt to acquire a portal site of its own. "The acquisition of XYZ.com," Meg Whitman announced, "will provide advertising revenues, will help us build the eBay brand, and will give us the size and clout we need to compete with larger sites like Amazon and Yahoo." The acquisition of XYZ.com comes on the heels of eBay's acquisition of two rising companies in the growing business-to-business auction market.

- *eBay broken up.* Like AT&T in the 1980s, and Microsoft a decade later, eBay's commanding market share attracts the unwanted attention of the U.S. Department of Justice (DOJ). "The network effect that has given eBay over 90 percent control of the person-to-person auction market, and a growing share of the business-to-business and to-consumer markets," said the DOJ complaint, "results in de facto monopolistic control over auction trade and user fees. Further, it represents an insurmountable barrier to competition." The DOJ aims for a breakup of eBay along market segment lines.

- *eBay chewed up by niche competitors.* By 2005, the eBay community had begun to break apart into balkanized regions. Many sellers in key high-priced categories (rare books, fine art, high-quality instruments, etc.) were moving their business to specialty auction sites, taking a chunk out of eBay's revenue growth.[4] "There is so much stuff, and so much cheap junk in my eBay category," one former eBay Power Seller complained, "that buyers weren't finding my listings. I was getting fewer and lower bids every month."

- *eBay displaced.* New technology makes it possible for individual manufacturers and even small businesses such as antique dealers to establish their own auction platforms. The newly developed software utility that makes this feasible, YourAuction, allows any business of any size to list auctions and complete transactions without intermediaries such as eBay and FastParts.com. A massive computer facility built and operated by a consortium of leading credit-card and financial institutions will connect all bidders and sellers.

- *eBay in steady state.* The New York Stock Exchange (NYSE), a nonprofit corporation, traces its origins to two dozen individuals who met regularly under a buttonwood tree in lower Manhattan in the early 1790s to trade government IOUs and bank shares. eBay, which has a similar informal origin, is following the NYSE's course of slow, incremental growth and development after an eight-year period of explosive growth. As the years go by its trading rules are becoming more refined and transparent to users; its trading volume grows in step with the national economy; and it is adjusting to greater regulation by the Federal Trade Commission. The incremental incorporation of new technology keeps it efficient and competitive with rival exchanges.

You can decide which of these scenarios is most likely. Of these possibilities, only "eBay displaced" is really bad for the company and its shareholders. Even a breakup may be an opportunity to sell off the parts of the business for more than they are worth individually. Shareholders of AT&T, you may recall, did very well when Ma Bell was taken apart in the 1980s.

Ironically, the greatest threat to the company's long-term prosperity may be the expectations of Wall Street and its own shareholders. Unreasonable expectations about continued future growth may tempt (or compel) eBay's executive team to tamper with its mission and the strategy that has supported it successfully to this point. If being the world's largest person-to-person online auction company is ever considered too narrow or too limiting, someone will be tempted to redirect the company and hope that the user community will follow. But as one long-time eBay watcher has noted, every time the company has listened to its users and followed their advice, it has succeeded. Every time it has tried to force changes on the user community, it has failed. This may be the most important lesson that eBay can learn from its own history.

In the end, eBay's managers should heed the advice of Sun Tzu in *The Art of War:* "To lead the people, walk behind them."

Notes

■ CHAPTER 1

1. See Maryann Jones Thompson, "Web Spotlight: The Hot Sites of 1999," *The Standard,* 20 December 1999.

2. See James Ledbetter, "The Internet Economy Gets Real," *The Standard,* 20 December 1999.

3. Terri Dougherty, "Oregon Goes Online," *eBay Magazine,* January 2000, pp. 76–77.

4. Evie Black Dykema, "Demand-Driven Pricing: More Sizzle than Steak," *Forrester Brief* (Forrester Research, Cambridge, MA), 20 September 1999, p. 2.

■ CHAPTER 2

1. Jim Collins, "Built to Flip," *Fast Company,* March 2000, pp. 131–143.

2. See Pierre Omidyar's introduction in Laura Fisher Kaiser and Michael Kaiser, *The Official eBay Guide* (New York: Fireside/Simon & Schuster, 1999), p. xv.

3. Kaiser and Kaiser, p. xv.

4. Based on 1998 estimates of the amounts spent through auctions and classified ads and on collectibles, per eBay's 10-K 1998, p. 4.

5. Interview with author, 11 February 2000.

6. William D. Bygrave and Jeffry A. Timmons, *Venture Capital at the Crossroads* (Boston: Harvard Business School Press, 1992), p. 224.

7. Bill Gates only stepped down as Microsoft's CEO in early 2000, but retained his position as board chairman.

8. Nicole Tempest, "Meg Whitman at eBay Inc. (A)," Case 9-400-035, revised 1 October 1999 (Boston: Harvard Business School Press), p. 3.

9. Susan Moran, "The Unknown," *Business 2.0,* June 1999.

■ CHAPTER 3

1. Chuck Lenatti, "Auction Mania," *Upside,* 4 June 1999.

2. Shaun Andrikopolous, "eBay Inc., Enabling an Army of Entrepreneurs—The Dominant On-Line Trading Community," BT Alex. Brown Research, 27 October 1998.

3. Nicole Tempest, "Meg Whitman at eBay Inc. (A)," Case 9-400-035, revised 1 October 1999 (Boston: Harvard Business School Press), pp. 5–6.

4. John Partinson. Interview with Richard Luecke, 23 December 1999.

5. The only disclosure of the reserve price is the parenthetical notation next to the current or starting price that states either "reserve not yet met" or "reserve met." The latter indicates that the current bid is above the seller's reserve price.

6. eBay refunds the insertion fee when reserve-price auctions are successfully consummated. It collects only the final value fee in these cases. Also, certain categories (vehicles and real estate) are charged fixed insertion and final fees.

7. From Andale press release, 5 October 1999.

8. Tempest, pp. 5–6.

9. From eBay User Agreement, November 1999.

10. Chuck Lenatti, "Auction Mania," *Upside,* 4 June 1999.

11. Tempest, p. 12.

12. Letter to the editor, *New York Times,* 9 March 2000.

13. Tempest, p. 15.

14. Heather Green, "The E.Biz 25," *BusinessWeek Online,* 27 September 1999.

15. Susan Moran, "The Candyman," *Business 2.0,* June 1999.

16. John Perry Barlow. Interview with author, 14 March 2000.

■ CHAPTER 4

1. Chuck Lenatti, "Auction Mania," *Upside,* 4 June 1999.

2. David Zale, *Sands Brothers Investment Research,* 28 December 1999, p. 1.

3. David Bovet and Joseph Martha, *Value Nets* (New York: John Wiley & Sons, 2000), p. 2.

4. See Ken Fisher, *Super Stocks* (Homewood, IL: Dow Jones Irwin, 1984).

5. Alfred Rappaport, "Ten Pointers for Investing in Internet Stocks," *Wall Street Journal,* 24 February 2000, p. R1.

6. Broadcast of *The Connection,* WBUR, Boston University, 3 April 2000.

7. Rappaport, p. R1.

8. As reported in Maryann Jones Thompson, "Analyst Insight: The Reality of Net Stock Valuations," *The Standard,* 18 October 1999.

■ CHAPTER 5

1. Po Bronson, *The Nudist on the Night Shift* (New York: Random House, 1999), p. xv.

2. Broadcast of *The Connection,* WBUR, Boston University, 3 April 2000.

3. Nicole Tempest, "Meg Whitman at eBay Inc. (A)," Case 9-400-035, revised 1 October 1999, (Boston: Harvard Business School Press), p. 7.

4. Tempest, p. 7.

5. See David Matheson and Jim Matheson, *The Smart Organization* (Boston: Harvard Business School Press, 1998).

6. Tempest, p. 7.

7. Tempest, p. 9.

8. Tempest, p. 9.

9. Chuck Lenatti, "Auction Mania," *Upside,* 4 June 1999.

10. Polly LaBarre, "Leaders.com," *Fast Company,* June 1999, p. 95.

11. Tempest, p. 17.

12. Tempest, p. 17.

13. "Web DNA," Russell Reynolds Associates Web site, 15 March 2000.

■ CHAPTER 6

1. eBay entered Japan via a joint venture with NEC. Under the terms of their agreement, NEC took an equity stake in eBay Japan and took responsibility for promoting the site through its Biglobe ISP, personal computer products, and offline marketing campaigns. Entry to the United Kingdom was built from the ground up. In Germany, the acquisition of alando.de.ag, a existing German trading service, provided eBay with a market foothold. Meanwhile, eBay entered Australia and New Zealand through a joint venture with a subsidiary of a major local media corporation.

2. David Aaker, *Managing Brand Equity* (New York: Free Press, 1991), p. 7.

3. Phil Carpenter, *eBrands* (Boston: Harvard Business School Press, 2000), p. 1.

4. Nicole Tempest, "Meg Whitman at eBay Inc. (A)," Case 9-400-035, revised 1 October 1999 (Boston: Harvard Business School Press), pp. 9–10.

5. Troy Wolverton, "eBay Latest to Tout Its E-business Ways," CNET News.com, 15 March 1999.

6. Tempest, p. 17.

■ CHAPTER 7

1. See Matt Richtel, "eBay Says Law Discourages Auction Monitoring," *New York Times,* 10 December 1999.

2. Nicole Tempest, "Meg Whitman at eBay Inc. (A)," Case 9-400-035, revised 1 October 1999 (Boston: Harvard Business School Press), p. 12.

3. Descriptions from individual auctions on the eBay Web site.

4. eBay Web site, 6 March 2000.

5. eBay Web site, 8 February 2000.

6. "Ebay Unscathed by Attacks," *Wired News* online, 24 February 2000.

7. Estimates by Bambi Francisco of CBS MarketWatch and George Anders of the *Wall Street Journal,* cited in "Ebay Spins Public Relations 101," *The Standard,* 14 June 1999.

8. See estimate in Maryann Jones Thompson, "Technology Spotlight: The Financial Impact of Site Outages, *The Standard,* 27 September 1999.

■ CHAPTER 8

1. Ed Ritchie, "The Fairmarket Approach," AuctionWatch.com., 20 October 1999.

2. From an AuctionWatch.com review of Amazon.com, 16 August 1999.

3. AuctionWatch.com.

4. "Amazon.com Makes a Market with Auctions," Keenan Vision Spot Analysis, 1 April 1999. www.kennan-scope.com.

5. See Rita Koselka, "A Real Amazon," *Forbes Global,* 5 April 1999.

6. Chuck Lenatti, "Auction Mania," *Upside,* 4 June 1999.

7. Lenatti.

8. Lenatti.

9. Linda Himelstein, "Interview with Meg Whitman," *BusinessWeek Online,* 31 May 1999.

10. Himelstein.

11. Jennifer Mack, *Inter@active Week,* 28 September 1999.

12. Penelope Patsuris, "Whither eBay," *Forbes,* 1 October 1999.

13. Lenatti.

14. AuctionWatch, Reviews, "Yahoo!"

■ CHAPTER 9

1. Bill Ghormley, *As Easy as Taking an Instant Picture: How Polaroid Employees Reengineered Customer Fulfillment.* (Cambridge, MA: Polaroid Corporation, 1993), pp. 3–4.

2. Bob Kagle. Interview with Richard Luecke, 11 February 2000.

3. Andy Roe, "Future Shock: Year 2000 Predictions for the Online Auction Industry," AuctionWatch daily features, 8 April 2000.

4. Thanks to Michael May of Jupiter Communications for suggesting this potential scenario.

Index